Julian Lindsay
September 10, 1935

B.H. Brockwell

D0876150

$ 2.00

SELECTED POETICAL WORKS
OF GEORGE MEREDITH

Works by
George Macaulay Trevelyan, O.M.

ENGLISH SOCIAL HISTORY

ILLUSTRATED ENGLISH SOCIAL HISTORY
> VOLUME I *Chaucer's England and the Early Tudors*
> VOLUME II *The Age of Shakespeare and the Stuart Period*
> VOLUME III *The Eighteenth Century*
> VOLUME IV *The Nineteenth Century*

HISTORY OF ENGLAND

BRITISH HISTORY IN THE NINETEENTH
> CENTURY AND AFTER (1782-1919)

ENGLAND UNDER QUEEN ANNE:
> *Blenheim*
> *Ramillies and the Union with Scotland*
> *The Peace and the Protestant Succession*

ENGLAND IN THE AGE OF WYCLIFFE

GREY OF FALLODON

GARIBALDI'S DEFENCE OF THE ROMAN REPUBLIC

GARIBALDI AND THE THOUSAND

GARIBALDI AND THE MAKING OF ITALY

LORD GREY OF THE REFORM BILL, THE LIFE OF
> CHARLES, SECOND EARL GREY

CLIO, A MUSE AND OTHER ESSAYS

AN AUTOBIOGRAPHY AND OTHER ESSAYS

A LAYMAN'S LOVE OF LETTERS

CARLYLE: AN ANTHOLOGY

GEORGE MEREDITH

from a sketch by Mortimer Menpes
in the possession of Captain G. W. L. Meredith

SELECTED
POETICAL WORKS OF
GEORGE MEREDITH

Compiled
with some Notes by

G. M. TREVELYAN, O.M.

Author of
'The Philosophy and Poetry of George Meredith'

LONGMANS, GREEN AND CO
LONDON   NEW YORK   TORONTO

LONGMANS, GREEN AND CO LTD
6 & 7 CLIFFORD STREET LONDON W I
BOSTON HOUSE STRAND STREET CAPE TOWN
531 LITTLE COLLINS STREET MELBOURNE

LONGMANS, GREEN AND CO INC
55 FIFTH AVENUE NEW YORK 3

LONGMANS, GREEN AND CO
20 CRANFIELD ROAD TORONTO 16

ORIENT LONGMANS LTD
CULCUTTA BOMBAY MADRAS
DELHI VIJAYAWADA DACCA

This Edition first Published 1955

Printed in Great Britain
by T. and A. CONSTABLE LTD., Hopetoun Street,
Printers to the University of Edinburgh

CONTENTS

(The dates indicate the year of first publication, in book or in periodical.)

vi *Contents*

INTRODUCTION

AT the moment that I write these words, Meredith's poems are all out of print, except *Modern Love* (Hart-Davis 1948). To remedy this deplorable state of things, I am here bringing out a selection amounting to about a third of the volume of his complete Poetical Works, which I edited for Messrs. Constable in 1912, now out of print. I have omitted two large classes of the collected poems ; first some hundred pages of Juvenilia which have little merit and little that is character-istic of Meredith ; and secondly a number of poems of his later years, which though highly characteristic of him are exceedingly difficult to understand,—such as *The Empty Purse*, *The Sage Enamoured*, and the Odes of French History all except the noble *France, December* 1870. One long and very difficult poem I have indeed retained, *The Woods of Westermain*, for the magical beauty of its opening, and many striking phrases scattered throughout its length.

I have retained from the volume of 1912 all my notes referring to those poems that are here reprinted. The notes are purely explanatory, and with their help I do not think that, except in the mazes of the *Woods of Westermain*, the reader should find any of the poems in this volume very difficult to understand.

Last year, in my *Layman's Love of Letters*, I wrote some-thing about Meredith as a poet. His reputation, both as novelist and poet, has had many ups and downs. He was born in 1828 and died at the age of eighty. In 1862 he pub-lished one of the greatest of his poems, the sonnet sequence of *Modern Love*. It was virulently attacked by the principal reviews as 'immoral,' because its subject was an unhappy marriage, though its treatment of that prohibited theme was serious, tragic and moral. These critics might at least as well have attacked as immoral another still more famous sonnet sequence, and they would no doubt have done so if it had been 'begotten' in their time. But indeed I think we may say of the author of *Modern Love* what he himself said of Shakespeare :

> He probed from hell to hell
> Of human passions, but of love deflowered
> His wisdom was not.

Swinburne, enraged at the folly of the critics, rushed into the fray, declaring the greatness of *Modern Love* as 'a poem above the aim and beyond the reach of any but its author.' But it was no use. Meredith was a condemned man, and for long years only a few friends paid attention either to his novels or to his poems, though *Harry Richmond* came out in 1871, and the final version of *Love in the Valley* in 1878. The utter neglect in which Meredith was left during the first and formative half of his life as an author had an unfortunate influence on his work. Since neither the critics not the public would listen to him, he soliloquized in prose and poetry, which became therefore increasingly eccentric and obscure. He once told me that as a young man he had hoped to be a popular novelist like Dickens, but soon found it to be impossible, and so wrote to please himself alone.

Recognition, though tardy, came at last. There were three distinct periods of the long Victorian age, and during the last of them, for twenty years before the Queen died, Meredith was regarded by a new and more enlightened generation of critics as an odd but a great man. Appreciation came first to his novels, on the publication of *The Egoist* in 1879. Its intellectual power and caprice, its humour and its psychology exactly suited the mental atmosphere of the 'eighties and 'nineties.

Meredith, in my opinion, had more intellectual power and finesse, and stronger imagination than any other of the Victorians, but neither in his novels nor in his poetry did he know how to employ them perfectly—except in some of his poems. His mental agility is very great, but it often leads him into a bog ; his poetical imagination never. For me, the best scenes in the novels are the most poetical, especially where the human situation is set in some aspect of nature : the crisis in the boat at sea under the Venetian Alps in chapter IX of *Beauchamp*, Vernon Whitford under the cherry tree, Diana's walk at dawn upon the mountain-side above Lugano—and a hundred more. His novels, no less than Hardy's, are the novels of a poet.

Recognition of Meredith as a poet followed slowly after his recognition as a novelist, partly because the new poems that he published in the 'eighties and 'nineties were many of them difficult and obscure, too heavily weighted with thought and with imagery imperfectly digested to be readable by ordinary mortals. I have left the more obscure poems out of this volume, but as a young man I studied them sedulously, and I am bound to say that I found them more interesting than the commonplaces that mainly compose the last half of the life's work of a greater poet, Wordsworth. I often visited Meredith at Box Hill, and in 1906 I published a book called *The Poetry and Philosophy of George Meredith*. It went through several editions and then died. *Requiescat in pace*. It was largely concerned with Meredith's poetical philosophy, his reading of Earth, in which he was more interested than in Heaven. But ideas date, while art survives. It is as a poet, not as a poetical philosopher, that he has claim to immortality.

In the last few years of his life, Meredith was regarded by many as the head of English letters. In 1898 Leslie Stephen forwarded to him a parchment bearing the good wishes of the authors of the day on his seventieth birthday, and ten years later his eightieth birthday was celebrated with even fuller honours. His friendly rival, Hardy, was generous in his praise, and wrote a beautiful poem on his death in 1909.

By that time much of his poetry was widely known and admired. Then came the First World War, and when we emerged from it his work in verse and prose no longer appealed to the new generation. He had sunk once more below the capricious horizon of literary fashion. But I rejoice to see that in our own latest age two of our poet-critics do full justice to his poetic powers. I refer to Mr. Siegfried Sassoon's *Meredith* (1948) and Mr. Day Lewis's edition of *Modern Love* of the same year with an introduction that leaves unsaid nothing that I would wish to say. After briefly telling the story of *Modern Love*, Mr. Day Lewis writes :

Such a summary gives little idea of the poem's dramatic movement, its skilful alternations of crisis with calm, tragic

necessity with lyrical illusion, cynicism or despair with
faith and tenderness ; nor of Meredith's quite extraordinary
psychological insight ; nor of the technical mastery which
enabled him both to transmute psychology into poetry and
to make the meditative sonnet form appear a perfectly apt
vehicle for a passionate monodrama.

Mr. Day Lewis has also said some very interesting things
about Meredith's use of the poetic image, in his well-known
Clark Lectures on that subject. Well, here is an instance of
an image from *Modern Love* (Sonnet XLIV p. 24 below).

> They say, that Pity in Love's service dwells,
> A porter at the rosy temple's gate.
> I missed him going : but it is my fate
> To come upon him now beside his wells ;
> Whereby I know that I Love's temple leave,
> And that the purple doors have closed behind.

I will only enforce the argument by directing special attention
to the Sixteenth Sonnet (p. 12) and the Fiftieth and last,
which has enriched our language with phrases often quoted,
sometimes by people who do not even know who their author
was.

The poem of Meredith's which first won the affection of
an appreciable number of readers, was of course *Love in the
Valley*. I remember that when I used to tell my friends, half
a century ago, that Meredith was a poet as well as a novelist,
one of them replied, ' O yes, he wrote *Love in the Valley* ; one
need not read anything else.' It is a poem of young love, set
in the south English countryside, following round the
farmer's year from the coming of one spring to the next. To
my thinking it is the most beautiful love poem of that length
to be found in our language. The first version of it, for
which I should certainly not advance any such claim, was
published in 1851, when he was twenty-three years old, and
still happily married to Peacock's daughter. Seven years later
she ran away from him. After that terrible experience, he
wrote *Modern Love* ; the relation of that poem to the actual
facts of his broken marriage has been treated by Mr. Day
Lewis in his Introduction, in a way on which I cannot improve.
Then more years passed, and Meredith, at the height of his

poetic powers, took up the first version of *Love in the Valley*,
which had the wonderful lilting metre, and some beautiful
lines, but was full also of juvenile weaknesses, some almost
puerile. (I have printed it in Appendix, p. 173 below.) Out
of this beginning, he produced as a middle-aged man the
Love in the Valley that we now have (pp. 81-87 below). He
changed the weak words and lines to strength or replaced
them altogether. And he more than doubled the length of
the poem. Yet it has not lost the freshness of the dawn of
young love when it is bliss to be alive, though a strain of
deeper poetry has been added to that theme. It is almost
impossible to choose out of the twenty-six stanzas any that
are more beautiful than the rest. The only charge that could
be made against the poem is monotony of feeling and beauty—
whereas *Modern Love* is distinguished for the variety of its
moods.

I know few things more interesting than the way in which
this early love poem of an enamoured boy was changed by
its author, twenty-five years later, from weakness to strength.

In *Love in the Valley* the purely human emotion is exalted
by the lover's contact with the beauties of Nature, and his
sense of Nature's underlying strength akin to mankind.
Meredith's philosophy of Earth was based on the fact that we
are literally her children. Sometimes he states this philosophy
of our kinship with earth too intellectually, but often it is an
unconscious but intrinsic element in his best poems such as :
*Earth and a Wedded Woman, Juggling Jerry, The Thrush in Feb-
ruary, Melampus, The Spirit of Earth in Autumn, Phoebus with
Admetus, The Day of the Daughter of Hades, Winter Heavens,
Dirge in Woods* and many more.

Meredith is poet of out of doors, by night and by day. He
spent much of his best years, before illness imprisoned his old
age, in long cross-country walks and in communion with
woods, fields and hills, with sun, wind and stars.

> I, who love old hymning night
> And know the dryad voices well.

> I know him, February's thrush,
> And loud at eve he valentines.

His walk in *The Orchard and the Heath, The Lark Ascending*,
the description of the nightingale's song in *Night of Frost in*

May all give a close observation of nature transfused into poetry in a way peculiarly his own.

But there is infinite variety in Meredith's moods and subjects. Besides his nature poems and his reading of earth, there are historical and patriotic poems, equally characteristic of him : *The Nuptials of Attila* (pp. 110-124) has a unique place for vigour among the historical picturings of poets.

And he had things of value to say about the affairs of his own day. He loved France, while he respected and feared Germany. Of both, as also of England, he was a most discerning critic. Of his four Odes on French History, the first in order of composition is by far the best and is the only one I have placed in this selection. It is called *France, December* 1870 (pp. 158-165) and was actually written and published while the German armies were overrunning prostrate France. The Ode is true poetry, and yet it is also a comment on the events of the day seen in their long historical setting.

Severe critic as he was of England, in her relations to Ireland and much else, he valued her for her real qualities and for her service to the world. If she fell, he wrote in 1908, ' mankind would breathe a harsher air.' Well, she has not fallen, but she has relatively declined, and the air is already more harsh. Meredith had received part of his schooling in Germany just before the era of Bismarck, and from the boyish experience he sensed much of the future. Already before 1870 he knew that the Germans would be our rivals, and dangerous rivals too, because they educated their people, which we then did not ; because they made long plans and carried them through ; and obeyed military rulers who believed in force. His mingled admiration and fear of the Germans come out in *Harry Richmond*, and the German chapters of it are well worth comparing with the very similar warning issued in the same year 1871 by Matthew Arnold in his *Friendship's Garland*. Though he was an advanced Liberal in other matters, Meredith believed that universal military service would prove the only means of preserving our island, anchored off a continent to whose real forces and tendencies we were shutting our eyes. See *To Colonel Charles* and *England before the Storm* (pp. 150-153). These and his two poems on Nelson (pp. 153-155) are among the fine things in our patriotic poetry.

A quality of Meredith's poems is their great variety, in theme, in mood, in metre. The strong crude lines of *The Nuptials of Attila* are in marked contrast to such poems as *Phoebus with Admetus* (pp. 74-77), *Lucifer in Starlight* and *The Star Sirius* (p. 38) or the little lyrics of nature like

> Sweet as Eden is the air,
>   And Eden-sweet the ray.
> No Paradise is lost for them
>   Who foot by branching root and stem,
> And lightly with the woodland share
>   The change of night and day.

and *Song in the Songless* (p. 168). Equally different is that unique *Hymn to Colour* (pp. 144-146), a poem difficult indeed, but rather for the mysticism of the feeling than for the over-intellectual character of the thought which militates against the poetic effect of much of his other work.

A dualism runs through the imagery of the *Hymn to Colour*. Light, Darkness and Colour answer to Life, Death and Love. Colour is to Light and Darkness as Love is to Life and Death. The poet, walking between Death and Life, is met by Love in the pale 'land of dawn,' between night and day, where dreams are floating fast to wreck on daylight.

> With Life and Death I walked when Love appeared,
> And made them on each side a shadow seem.

Meredith's poems have meant so much to me all through my life. My object in producing this selection is to enable other lovers of poetry to judge if he can mean anything to them.

G. M. TREVELYAN.

June 1954.

NOTE

AN asterisk after the title of a poem indicates
that there is a note on it at the end of the book,
the note referring either to the poem as a whole,
or to some special passage indicated in the text
by a numeral.

POEMS

JUGGLING JERRY

I

PITCH here the tent, while the old horse grazes :
    By the old hedge-side we'll halt a stage.
It's nigh my last above the daisies :
    My next leaf'll be man's blank page.
Yes, my old girl ! and it's no use crying :
    Juggler, constable, king, must bow.
One that outjuggles all's been spying
    Long to have me, and he has me now.

II

We've travelled times to this old common :
    Often we've hung our pots in the gorse.
We've had a stirring life, old woman,
    You, and I, and the old grey horse.
Races, and fairs, and royal occasions,
    Found us coming to their call :
Now they'll miss us at our stations :
    There's a Juggler outjuggles all !

III

Up goes the lark, as if all were jolly !
    Over the duck-pond the willow shakes.
Easy to think that grieving's folly,
    When the hand's firm as driven stakes !
Ay, when we're strong, and braced, and manful,
    Life's a sweet fiddle : but we're a batch
Born to become the Great Juggler's han'ful :
    Balls he shies up, and is safe to catch.

IV

Here's where the lads of the village cricket :
   I was a lad not wide from here :
Couldn't I whip off the bail from the wicket ?
   Like an old world those days appear !
Donkey, sheep, geese, and thatched ale-house—I
      know them !
   They are old friends of my halts, and seem,
Somehow, as if kind thanks I owe them :
   Juggling don't hinder the heart's esteem.

V

Juggling's no sin, for we must have victual :
   Nature allows us to bait for the fool.
Holding one's own makes us juggle no little ;
   But, to increase it, hard juggling's the rule.
You that are sneering at my profession,
   Haven't you juggled a vast amount ?
There's the Prime Minister, in one Session,
   Juggles more games than my sins'll count.

VI

I've murdered insects with mock thunder :
   Conscience, for that, in men don't quail.
I've made bread from the bump of wonder :
   That's my business, and there's my tale.
Fashion and rank all praised the professor :
   Ay ! and I've had my smile from the Queen :
Bravo, Jerry ! she meant : God bless her !
   Ain't this a sermon on that scene ?

VII

I've studied men from my topsy-turvy
   Close, and, I reckon, rather true.
Some are fine fellows : some, right scurvy
   Most, a dash between the two.
But it's a woman, old girl, that makes me
   Think more kindly of the race :
And it's a woman, old girl, that shakes me
   When the Great Juggler I must face.

VIII

We two were married, due and legal :
   Honest we've lived since we've been one.
Lord ! I could then jump like an eagle :
   You danced bright as a bit o' the sun.
Birds in a May-bush we were ! right merry !
   All night we kiss'd, we juggled all day.
Joy was the heart of Juggling Jerry !
   Now from his old girl he's juggled away.

IX

It's past parsons to console us :
   No, nor no doctor fetch for me :
I can die without my bolus ;
   Two of a trade, lass, never agree !
Parson and Doctor !—don't they love rarely
   Fighting the devil in other men's fields !
Stand up yourself and match him fairly :
   Then see how the rascal yields !

X

I, lass, have lived no gipsy, flaunting
   Finery while his poor helpmate grubs :
Coin I've stored, and you won't be wanting :
   You shan't beg from the troughs and tubs.
Nobly you've stuck to me, though in his kitchen
   Many a Marquis would hail you Cook !
Palaces you could have ruled and grown rich in,
   But your old Jerry you never forsook.

XI

Hand up the chirper ! ripe ale winks in it ;
   Let's have comfort and be at peace.
Once a stout draught made me light as a linnet.
   Cheer up ! the Lord must have his lease.
May be—for none see in that black hollow—
   It's just a place where we're held in pawn,
And, when the Great Juggler makes as to swallow,
   It's just the sword-trick—I ain't quite gone !

B

XII

Yonder came smells of the gorse, so nutty,
  Gold-like and warm : it's the prime of May.
Better than mortar, brick and putty
  Is God's house on a blowing day.
Lean me more up the mound ; now I feel it :
  All the old heath-smells ! Ain't it strange ?
There's the world laughing, as if to conceal it,
  But He's by us, juggling the change.

XIII

I mind it well, by the sea-beach lying,
  Once—it's long gone—when two gulls we beheld,
Which, as the moon got up, were flying
  Down a big wave that sparked and swelled.
Crack, went a gun : one fell : the second
  Wheeled round him twice, and was off for new luck :
There in the dark her white wing beckon'd :—
  Drop me a kiss—I'm the bird dead-struck !

BY THE ROSANNA

TO F. M.

STANZER THAL, TYROL.

THE old grey Alp has caught the cloud,
And the torrent river sings aloud ;
The glacier-green Rosanna sings
An organ song of its upper springs.
Foaming under the tiers of pine,
I see it dash down the dark ravine,
And it tumbles the rocks in boisterous play,
With an earnest will to find its way.
Sharp it throws out an emerald shoulder,
    And, thundering ever of the mountain,
Slaps in sport some giant boulder,
    And tops it in a silver fountain.

A chain of foam from end to end,
And a solitude so deep, my friend,
You may forget that man abides
Beyond the great mute mountain-sides.
Yet to me, in this high-walled solitude
Of river and rock and forest rude,
The roaring voice through the long white chain
Is the voice of the world of bubble and brain.

THE PROMISE IN DISTURBANCE *

How low when angels fall their black descent,
Our primal thunder tells : known is the pain
Of music, that nigh throning wisdom went,
And one false note cast wailful to the insane.
Now seems the language heard of Love as rain
To make a mire where fruitfulness was meant.
The golden harp gives out a jangled strain,
Too like revolt from heaven's Omnipotent.
But listen in the thought ; so may there come
Conception of a newly-added chord,
Commanding space beyond where ear has home.
In labour of the trouble at its fount,
Leads Life to an intelligible Lord
The rebel discords up the sacred mount.

MODERN LOVE *

I *

BY this he knew she wept with waking eyes :
That, at his hand's light quiver by her head,
The strange low sobs that shook their common bed
Were called into her with a sharp surprise,
And strangled mute, like little gaping snakes,
Dreadfully venomous to him. She lay
Stone-still, and the long darkness flowed away
With muffled pulses. Then, as midnight makes

Her giant heart of Memory and Tears
Drink the pale drug of silence, and so beat
Sleep's heavy measure, they from head to feet
Were moveless, looking through their dead black years,
By vain regret scrawled over the blank wall.
Like sculptured effigies they might be seen
Upon their marriage-tomb, the sword between ;
Each wishing for the sword that severs all.

II

It ended, and the morrow brought the task.
Her eyes were guilty gates, that let him in
By shutting all too zealous for their sin :
Each sucked a secret, and each wore a mask.
But, oh, the bitter taste her beauty had !
He sickened as at breath of poison-flowers :
A languid humour stole among the hours,
And if their smiles encountered, he went mad,
And raged deep inward, till the light was brown
Before his vision, and the world, forgot,
Looked wicked as some old dull murder-spot.
A star with lurid beams, she seemed to crown
The pit of infamy : and then again
He fainted on his vengefulness, and strove
To ape the magnanimity of love,
And smote himself, a shuddering heap of pain.

III *

This was the woman ; what now of the man ?
But pass him. If he comes beneath a heel,
He shall be crushed until he cannot feel,
Or, being callous, haply till he can.
But he is nothing :—nothing ? Only mark
The rich light striking out from her on him !
Ha ! what a sense it is when her eyes swim
Across the man she singles, leaving dark
All else ! Lord God, who mad'st the thing so fair,
See that I am drawn to her even now !
It cannot be such harm on her cool brow
To put a kiss ? Yet if I meet him there !

But she is mine ! Ah, no ! I know too well
I claim a star whose light is overcast :
I claim a phantom-woman in the Past.
The hour has struck, though I heard not the bell !

iv *

All other joys of life he strove to warm,
And magnify, and catch them to his lip :
But they had suffered shipwreck with the ship,
And gazed upon him sallow from the storm.
Or if Delusion came, 'twas but to show
The coming minute mock the one that went.
Cold as a mountain in its star-pitched tent,
Stood high Philosophy, less friend than foe :
Whom self-caged Passion, from its prison-bars,
Is always watching with a wondering hate.
Not till the fire is dying in the grate,
Look we for any kinship with the stars.
Oh, wisdom never comes when it is gold,
And the great price we pay for it full worth :
We have it only when we are half earth.
Little avails that coinage to the old !

v *

A message from her set his brain aflame.
A world of household matters filled her mind,
Wherein he saw hypocrisy designed :
She treated him as something that is tame,
And but at other provocation bites.
Familiar was her shoulder in the glass,
Through that dark rain : yet it may come to pass
That a changed eye finds such familiar sights
More keenly tempting than new loveliness.
The ' What has been ' a moment seemed his own :
The splendours, mysteries, dearer because known,
Nor less divine : Love's inmost sacredness
Called to him, ' Come ! '—In his restraining start,
Eyes nurtured to be looked at scarce could see
A wave of the great waves of Destiny
Convulsed at a checked impulse of the heart.

VI *

It chanced his lips did meet her forehead cool.
She had no blush, but slanted down her eye.
Shamed nature, then, confesses love can die :
And most she punishes the tender fool
Who will believe what honours her the most !
Dead ! is it dead ? She has a pulse, and flow
Of tears, the price of blood-drops, as I know,
For whom the midnight sobs around Love's ghost,
Since then I heard her, and so will sob on.
The love is here ; it has but changed its aim.
O bitter barren woman ! what's the name ?
The name, the name, the new name thou hast won ?
Behold me striking the world's coward stroke !
That will I not do, though the sting is dire.
—Beneath the surface this, while by the fire
They sat, she laughing at a quiet joke.

VII *

She issues radiant from her dressing-room,
Like one prepared to scale an upper sphere :
—By stirring up a lower, much I fear !
How deftly that oiled barber lays his bloom !
That long-shanked dapper Cupid with frisked curls
Can make known women torturingly fair ;
The gold-eyed serpent dwelling in rich hair
Awakes beneath his magic whisks and twirls.
His art can take the eyes from out my head,
Until I see with eyes of other men ;
While deeper knowledge crouches in its den,
And sends a spark up :—is it true we are wed ?
Yea ! filthiness of body is most vile,
But faithlessness of heart I do hold worse.
The former, it were not so great a curse
To read on the steel-mirror of her smile.

VIII *

Yet it was plain she struggled, and that salt
Of righteous feeling made her pitiful.
Poor twisting worm, so queenly beautiful !
Where came the cleft between us ? whose the fault ?

My tears are on thee, that have rarely dropped
As balm for any bitter wound of mine :
My breast will open for thee at a sign !
But, no : we are two reed-pipes, coarsely stopped :
The God once filled them with his mellow breath ;
And they were music till he flung them down,
Used ! used ! Hear now the discord-loving clown
Puff his gross spirit in them, worse than death !
I do not know myself without thee more :
In this unholy battle I grow base :
If the same soul be under the same face,
Speak, and a taste of that old time restore !

IX *

He felt the wild beast in him betweenwhiles
So masterfully rude, that he would grieve
To see the helpless delicate thing receive
His guardianship through certain dark defiles.
Had he not teeth to rend, and hunger too ?
But still he spared her. Once : ' Have you no fear ? '
He said : 'twas dusk ; she in his grasp ; none near
She laughed : ' No, surely ; am I not with you ? '
And uttering that soft starry ' you,' she leaned
Her gentle body near him, looking up ;
And from her eyes, as from a poison-cup,
He drank until the flittering eyelids screened.
Devilish malignant witch ! and oh, young beam
Of heaven's circle-glory ! Here thy shape
To squeeze like an intoxicating grape—
I might, and yet thou goest safe, supreme.

X *

But where began the change ; and what's my crime ?
The wretch condemned, who has not been arraigned,
Chafes at his sentence. Shall I, unsustained,
Drag on Love's nerveless body thro' all time ?
I must have slept, since now I wake. Prepare,
You lovers, to know Love a thing of moods :
Not, like hard life, of laws. In Love's deep woods,
I dreamt of loyal Life :—the offence is there !

Love's jealous woods about the sun are curled ;
At least, the sun far brighter there did beam.—
My crime is, that the puppet of a dream,
I plotted to be worthy of the world.
Oh, had I with my darling helped to mince
The facts of life, you still had seen me go
With hindward feather and with forward toe,
Her much-adored delightful Fairy Prince !

XI

Out in the yellow meadows, where the bee
Hums by us with the honey of the Spring,
And showers of sweet notes from the larks on wing
Are dropping like a noon-dew, wander we.
Or is it now ? or was it then ? for now,
As then, the larks from running rings pour showers :
The golden foot of May is on the flowers,
And friendly shadows dance upon her brow.
What's this, when Nature swears there is no change
To challenge eyesight ? Now, as then, the grace
Of heaven seems holding earth in its embrace.
Nor eyes, nor heart, has she to feel it strange ?
Look, woman, in the West. There wilt thou see
An amber cradle near the sun's decline :
Within it, featured even in death divine,
Is lying a dead infant, slain by thee.

XII

Not solely that the Future she destroys,
And the fair life which in the distance lies
For all men, beckoning out from dim rich skies :
Nor that the passing hour's supporting joys
Have lost the keen-edged flavour, which begat
Distinction in old times, and still should breed
Sweet Memory, and Hope,—earth's modest seed,
And heaven's high-prompting : not that the world is flat
Since that soft-luring creature I embraced
Among the children of Illusion went :
Methinks with all this loss I were content,
If the mad Past, on which my foot is based,

Were firm, or might be blotted : but the whole
Of life is mixed : the mocking Past will stay :
And if I drink oblivion of a day,
So shorten I the stature of my soul.

XIII *

' I play for Seasons ; not Eternities ! '
Says Nature, laughing on her way. ' So must
All those whose stake is nothing more than dust ! '
And lo, she wins, and of her harmonies
She is full sure ! Upon her dying rose
She drops a look of fondness, and goes by,
Scarce any retrospection in her eye ;
For she the laws of growth most deeply knows,
Whose hands bear, here, a seed-bag—there, an urn.
Pledged she herself to aught, 'twould mark her end !
This lesson of our only visible friend
Can we not teach our foolish hearts to learn ?
Yes ! yes !—but, oh, our human rose is fair
Surpassingly ! Lose calmly Love's great bliss,
When the renewed for ever of a kiss
Whirls life within the shower of loosened hair !

XIV *

What soul would bargain for a cure that brings
Contempt the nobler agony to kill ?
Rather let me bear on the bitter ill,
And strike this rusty bosom with new stings !
It seems there is another veering fit,
Since on a gold-haired lady's eyeballs pure
I looked with little prospect of a cure,
The while her mouth's red bow loosed shafts of wit.
Just heaven ! can it be true that jealousy
Has decked the woman thus ? and does her head
Swim somewhat for possessions forfeited ?
Madam, you teach me many things that be.
I open an old book, and there I find
That ' Woman still may love whom they deceive.'
Such love I prize not, madam : by your leave,
The game you play at is not to my mind.

XV *

I think she sleeps : it must be sleep, when low
Hangs that abandoned arm toward the floor ;
The face turned with it. Now make fast the door.
Sleep on : it is your husband, not your foe.
The Poet's black stage-lion of wronged love
Frights not our modern dames :—well if he did !
Now will I pour new light upon that lid,
Full-sloping like the breasts beneath. ' Sweet dove,
Your sleep is pure. Nay, pardon : I disturb.
I do not ? good ! ' Her waking infant-stare
Grows woman to the burden my hands bear :
Her own handwriting to me when no curb
Was left on Passion's tongue. She trembles through ;
A woman's tremble—the whole instrument :—
I show another letter lately sent.
The words are very like : the name is new.

XVI

In our old shipwrecked days there was an hour,
When in the firelight steadily aglow,
Joined slackly, we beheld the red chasm grow
Among the clicking coals. Our library-bower
That eve was left to us : and hushed we sat
As lovers to whom Time is whispering.
From sudden-opened doors we heard them sing :
The nodding elders mixed good wine with chat.
Well knew we that Life's greatest treasure lay
With us, and of it was our talk. ' Ah, yes !
Love dies ! ' I said : I never thought it less.
She yearned to me that sentence to unsay.
Then when the fire domed blackening, I found
Her cheek was salt against my kiss, and swift
Up the sharp scale of sobs her breast did lift :—
Now am I haunted by that taste ! that sound !

XVII

At dinner, she is hostess, I am host.
Went the feast ever cheerfuller ? She keeps
The Topic over intellectual deeps
In buoyancy afloat. They see no ghost.

With sparkling surface-eyes we ply the ball :
It is in truth a most contagious game :
HIDING THE SKELETON, shall be its name.
Such play as this the devils might appal !
But here's the greater wonder ; in that we,
Enamoured of an acting nought can tire,
Each other, like true hypocrites, admire ;
Warm-lighted looks, Love's ephemerioe,
Shoot gaily o'er the dishes and the wine.
We waken envy of our happy lot.
Fast, sweet, and golden, shows the marriage-knot.
Dear guests, you now have seen Love's corpse-light shine.

XVIII *

Here Jack and Tom are paired with Moll and Meg.
Curved open to the river-reach is seen
A country merry-making on the green.
Fair space for signal shakings of the leg.
That little screwy fiddler from his booth,
Whence flows one nut-brown stream, commands the
      joints
Of all who caper here at various points.
I have known rustic revels in my youth :
The May-fly pleasures of a mind at ease.
An early goddess was a country lass :
A charmed Amphion-oak she tripped the grass.
What life was that I lived ? The life of these ?
Heaven keep them happy ! Nature they seem near.
They must, I think, be wiser than I am ;
They have the secret of the bull and lamb.
'Tis true that when we trace its source, 'tis beer.

XIX

No state is enviable. To the luck alone
Of some few favoured men I would put claim.
I bleed, but her who wounds I will not blame.
Have I not felt her heart as 'twere my own
Beat thro' me ? could I hurt her ? heaven and hell !
But I could hurt her cruelly ! Can I let
My Love's old time-piece to another set,
Swear it can't stop, and must for ever swell ?

Sure, that's one way Love drifts into the mart
Where goat-legged buyers throng. I see not plain :—
My meaning is, it must not be again.
Great God ! the maddest gambler throws his heart.
If any state be enviable on earth,
'Tis yon born idiot's, who, as days go by,
Still rubs his hands before him, like a fly,
In a queer sort of meditative mirth.

xx

I am not of those miserable males
Who sniff at vice, and, daring not to snap,
Do therefore hope for heaven. I take the hap
Of all my deeds. The wind that fills my sails
Propels ; but I am helmsman. Am I wrecked,
I know the devil has sufficient weight
To bear : I lay it not on him, or fate.
Besides, he's damned. That man I do suspect
A coward, who would burden the poor deuce
With what ensues from his own slipperiness.
I have just found a wanton-scented tress
In an old desk, dusty for lack of use.
Of days and nights it is demonstrative,
That, like some aged star, gleam luridly.
If for those times I must ask charity,
Have I not any charity to give ?

xxi

We three are on the cedar-shadowed lawn ;
My friend being third.   He who at love once laughed
Is in the weak rib by a fatal shaft
Struck through, and tells his passion's bashful dawn
And radiant culmination, glorious crown,
When ' this ' she said : went ' thus ' : most wondrous
      she.
Our eyes grow white, encountering : that we are three,
Forgetful ; then together we look down.
But he demands our blessing ; is convinced
That words of wedded lovers must bring good.
We question ; if we dare ! or if we should !
And pat him, with light laugh. We have not winced.

Next, she has fallen. Fainting points the sign
To happy things in wedlock. When she wakes,
She looks the star that thro' the cedar shakes :
Her lost moist hand clings mortally to mine.

XXII

What may the woman labour to confess ?
There is about her mouth a nervous twitch.
'Tis something to be told, or hidden :—which ?
I get a glimpse of hell in this mild guess.
She has desires of touch, as if to feel
That all the household things are things she knew.
She stops before the glass. What sight in view ?
A face that seems the latest to reveal !
For she turns from it hastily, and tossed
Irresolute steals shadow-like to where
I stand ; and wavering pale before me there,
Her tears fall still as oak-leaves after frost.
She will not speak. I will not ask. We are
League-sundered by the silent gulf between.
You burly lovers on the village green,
Yours is a lower, and a happier star !

XXIII

'Tis Christmas weather, and a country house
Receives us : rooms are full : we can but get
An attic-crib. Such lovers will not fret
At that, it is half-said. The great carouse
Knocks hard upon the midnight's hollow door,
But when I knock at hers, I see the pit.
Why did I come here in that dullard fit ?
I enter, and lie couched upon the floor.
Passing, I caught the coverlet's quick beat :—
Come, Shame, burn to my soul ! and Pride, and Pain—
Foul demons that have tortured me, enchain !
Out in the freezing darkness the lambs bleat.
The small bird stiffens in the low starlight.
I know not how, but shuddering as I slept,
I dreamed a banished angel to me crept :
My feet were nourished on her breasts all night.

XXIV

The misery is greater, as I live !
To know her flesh so pure, so keen her sense,
That she does penance now for no offence,
Save against Love. The less can I forgive !
The less can I forgive, though I adore
That cruel lovely pallor which surrounds
Her footsteps ; and the low vibrating sounds
That come on me, as from a magic shore.
Low are they, but most subtle to find out
The shrinking soul. Madam, 'tis understood
When women play upon their womanhood,
It means, a Season gone. And yet I doubt
But I am duped. That nun-like look waylays
My fancy. Oh ! I do but wait a sign !
Pluck out the eyes of pride ! thy mouth to mine !
Never ! though I die thirsting. Go thy ways !

XXV

You like not that French novel ? Tell me why.
You think it quite unnatural. Let us see.
The actors are, it seems, the usual three :
Husband, and wife, and lover. She—but fie !
In England we'll not hear of it. Edmond,
The lover, her devout chagrin doth share ;
Blanc-mange and absinthe are his penitent fare,
Till his pale aspect makes her over-fond :
So, to preclude fresh sin, he tries rosbif.
Meantime the husband is no more abused :
Auguste forgives her ere the tear is used.
Then hangeth all on one tremendous If :—
If she will choose between them. She does choose ;
And takes her husband, like a proper wife.
Unnatural ? My dear, these things are life :
And life, some think, is worthy of the Muse.

XXVI

Love ere he bleeds, an eagle in high skies,
Has earth beneath his wings : from reddened eve
He views the rosy dawn. In vain they weave
The fatal web below while far he flies.

But when the arrow strikes him, there's a change.
He moves but in the track of his spent pain,
Whose red drops are the links of a harsh chain,
Binding him to the ground, with narrow range.
A subtle serpent then has Love become.
I had the eagle in my bosom erst :
Henceforward with the serpent I am cursed.
I can interpret where the mouth is dumb.
Speak, and I see the side-lie of a truth.
Perchance my heart may pardon you this deed :
But be no coward :—you that made Love bleed,
You must bear all the venom of his tooth !

XXVII *

Distraction is the panacea, Sir !
I hear my oracle of Medicine say.
Doctor ! that same specific yesterday
I tried, and the result will not deter
A second trial. Is the devil's line
Of golden hair, or raven black, composed ?
And does a cheek, like any sea-shell rosed,
Or clear as widowed sky, seem most divine ?
No matter, so I taste forgetfulness.
And if the devil snare me, body and mind,
Here gratefully I score :—he seemëd kind,
When not a soul would comfort my distress !
O sweet new world, in which I rise new made !
O Lady, once I gave love : now I take !
Lady, I must be flattered. Shouldst thou wake
The passion of a demon, be not afraid.

XXVIII

I must be flattered. The imperious
Desire speaks out. Lady, I am content
To play with you the game of Sentiment,
And with you enter on paths perilous ;
But if across your beauty I throw light,
To make it threefold, it must be all mine.
First secret ; then avowed. For I must shine
Envied,—I, lessened in my proper sight !

Be watchful of your beauty, Lady dear !
How much hangs on that lamp you cannot tell.
Most earnestly I pray you, tend it well :
And men shall see me as a burning sphere ;
And men shall mark you eyeing me, and groan
To be the God of such a grand sunflower !
I feel the promptings of Satanic power,
While you do homage unto me alone.

XXIX

Am I failing ? For no longer can I cast
A glory round about this head of gold.
Glory she wears, but springing from the mould ;
Not like the consecration of the Past !
Is my soul beggared ? Something more than earth
I cry for still : I cannot be at peace
In having Love upon a mortal lease.
I cannot take the woman at her worth !
Where is the ancient wealth wherewith I clothed
Our human nakedness, and could endow
With spiritual splendour a white brow
That else had grinned at me the fact I loathed ?
A kiss is but a kiss now ! and no wave
Of a great flood that whirls me to the sea.
But, as you will ! we'll sit contentedly,
And eat our pot of honey on the grave.

XXX *

What are we first ? First, animals ; and next
Intelligences at a leap ; on whom
Pale lies the distant shadow of the tomb,
And all that draweth on the tomb for text.
Into which state comes Love, the crowning sun :
Beneath whose light the shadow loses form.
We are the lords of life, and life is warm.
Intelligence and instinct now are one.
But nature says : ' My children most they seem
When they least know me : therefore I decree
That they shall suffer.' Swift doth young Love flee,
And we stand wakened, shivering from our dream.

Then if we study Nature we are wise.
Thus do the few who live but with the day :
The scientific animals are they.—
Lady, this is my sonnet to your eyes.

XXXI

This golden head has wit in it. I live
Again, and a far higher life, near her.
Some women like a young philosopher ;
Perchance because he is diminutive.
For woman's manly god must not exceed
Proportions of the natural nursing size.
Great poets and great sages draw no prize
With women : but the little lap-dog breed,
Who can be hugged, or on a mantel-piece
Perched up for adoration, these obtain
Her homage. And of this we men are vain ?
Of this ! 'Tis ordered for the world's increase !
Small flattery ! Yet she has that rare gift
To beauty, Common Sense. I am approved.
It is not half so nice as being loved,
And yet I do prefer it. What's my drift ?

XXXII

Full faith I have she holds that rarest gift
To beauty, Common Sense. To see her lie
With her fair visage an inverted sky
Bloom-covered, while the underlids uplift,
Would almost wreck the faith ; but when her mouth
(Can it kiss sweetly ? sweetly !) would address
The inner me that thirsts for her no less,
And has so long been languishing in drouth,
I feel that I am matched ; that I am man !
One restless corner of my heart or head,
That holds a dying something never dead,
Still frets, though Nature giveth all she can.
It means, that woman is not, I opine,
Her sex's antidote. Who seeks the asp
For serpents' bites ? 'Twould calm me could I clasp
Shrieking Bacchantes with their souls of wine !

c

XXXIII *

' In Paris, at the Louvre, there have I seen
The sumptuously-feathered angel pierce
Prone Lucifer, descending. Looked he fierce,
Showing the fight a fair one ? Too serene !
The young Pharsalians did not disarray
Less willingly their locks of floating silk :
That suckling mouth of his upon the milk
Of heaven might still be feasting through the fray.
Oh, Raphael ! when men the Fiend do fight,
They conquer not upon such easy terms.
Half serpent in the struggle grow these worms.
And does he grow half human, all is right.'
This to my Lady in a distant spot,
Upon the theme : *While mind is mastering clay,*
Gross clay invades it. If the spy you play,
My wife, read this ! Strange love-talk, is it not ?

XXXIV *

Madam would speak with me. So, now it comes :
The deluge or else Fire ! She's well ; she thanks
My husbandship. Our chain on silence clanks.
Time leers between, above his twiddling thumbs.
Am I quite well ? Most excellent in health !
The journals, too, I diligently peruse.
Vesuvius is expected to give news :
Niagara is no noisier. By stealth
Our eyes dart scrutinizing snakes. She's glad
I'm happy, says her quivering under-lip.
' And are not you ? ' ' How can I be ? ' ' Take ship !
For happiness is somewhere to be had.'
' Nowhere for me ! ' Her voice is barely heard.
I am not melted, and make no pretence.
With commonplace I freeze her, tongue and sense.
Niagara or Vesuvius is deferred.

XXXV

It is no vulgar nature I have wived.
Secretive, sensitive, she takes a wound
Deep to her soul, as if the sense had swooned,
And not a thought of vengeance had survived.

No confidences has she : but relief
Must come to one whose suffering is acute.
O have a care of natures that are mute !
They punish you in acts : their steps are brief.
What is she doing ? What does she demand
From Providence or me ? She is not one
Long to endure this torpidly, and shun
The drugs that crowd about a woman's hand.
At Forfeits during snow we played, and I
Must kiss her. ' Well performed ! ' I said : then she :
' 'Tis hardly worth the money, you agree ? '
Save her ? What for ? To act this wedded lie !

XXXVI

My Lady unto Madam makes her bow.
The charm of women is, that even while
You're probed by them for tears, you yet may smile,
Nay, laugh outright, as I have done just now.
The interview was gracious : they anoint
(To me aside) each other with fine praise :
Discriminating compliments they raise,
That hit with wondrous aim on the weak point :
My Lady's nose of Nature might complain.
It is not fashioned aptly to express
Her character of large-browed steadfastness.
But Madam says : Thereof she may be vain !
Now, Madam's faulty feature is a glazed
And inaccessible eye, that has soft fires,
Wide gates, at love-time, only. This admires
My Lady. At the two I stand amazed.

XXXVII

Along the garden terrace, under which
A purple valley (lighted at its edge
By smoky torch-flame on the long cloud-ledge
Whereunder dropped the chariot) glimmers rich,
A quiet company we pace and wait,
The dinner-bell in prae-digestive calm.
So sweet up violet banks the Southern balm
Breathes round, we care not if the bell be late :

Though here and there grey seniors question Time
In irritable coughings. With slow foot
The low rosed moon, the face of Music mute,
Begins among her silent bars to climb.
As in and out, in silvery dusk, we thread,
I hear the laugh of Madam, and discern
My Lady's heel before me at each turn.
Our tragedy, is it alive or dead ?

XXXVIII *

Give to imagination some pure light
In human form to fix it, or you shame
The devils with that hideous human game :—
Imagination urging appetite !
Thus fallen have earth's greatest Gogmagogs,
Who dazzle us, whom we can not revere :
Imagination is the charioteer
That, in default of better, drives the hogs.
So, therefore, my dear Lady, let me love !
My soul is arrowy to the light in you.
You know me that I never can renew
The bond that woman broke : what would you have ?
'Tis Love, or Vileness ! not a choice between,
Save petrifaction ! What does Pity here ?
She killed a thing, and now it's dead, 'tis dear.
Oh, when you counsel me, think what you mean !

XXXIX *

She yields : my Lady in her noblest mood
Has yielded : she, my golden-crownëd rose !
The bride of every sense ! more sweet than those
Who breathe the violet breath of maidenhood.
O visage of still music in the sky !
Soft moon ! I feel thy song, my fairest friend !
True harmony within can apprehend
Dumb harmony without. And hark ! 'tis nigh !
Belief has struck the note of sound : a gleam
Of living silver shows me where she shook
Her long white fingers down the shadowy brook,
That sings her song, half waking, half in dream.

What two come here to mar this heavenly tune ?
A man is one : the woman bears my name,
And honour. Their hands touch ! Am I still tame ?
God, what a dancing spectre seems the moon !

XL *

I bade my Lady think what she might mean.
Know I my meaning, I ? Can I love one,
And yet be jealous of another ? None
Commits such folly. Terrible Love, I ween,
Has might, even dead, half sighing to upheave
The lightless seas of selfishness amain :
Seas that in a man's heart have no rain
To fall and still them. Peace can I achieve,
By turning to this fountain-source of woe,
This woman, who's to Love as fire to wood ?
She breathed the violet breath of maidenhood
Against my kisses once ! but I say, No !
The thing is mocked at ! Helplessly afloat,
I know not what I do, whereto I strive.
The dread that my old love may be alive
Has seized my nursling new love by the throat.

XLI *

How many a thing which we cast to the ground,
When others pick it up becomes a gem !
We grasp at all the wealth it is to them ;
And by reflected light its worth is found.
Yet for us still 'tis nothing ! and that zeal
Of false appreciation quickly fades.
This truth is little known to human shades,
. How rare from their own instinct 'tis to feel !
They waste the soul with spurious desire,
That is not the ripe flame upon the bough.
We two have taken up a lifeless vow
To rob a living passion : dust for fire !
Madam is grave, and eyes the clock that tells
Approaching midnight. We have struck despair
Into two hearts. O, look we like a pair
Who for fresh nuptials joyfully yield all else ?

XLII *

I am to follow her. There is much grace
In women when thus bent on martyrdom.
They think that dignity of soul may come,
Perchance, with dignity of body. Base !
But I was taken by that air of cold
And statuesque sedateness, when she said
' I'm going ' ; lit a taper, bowed her head,
And went, as with the stride of Pallas bold.
Fleshly indifference horrible ! The hands
Of Time now signal : O, she's safe from me !
Within those secret walls what do I see ?
Where first she set the taper down she stands :
Not Pallas : Hebe shamed ! Thoughts black as death
Like a stirred pool in sunshine break. Her wrists
I catch : she faltering, as she half-resists,
' You love . . . ? love . . . ? love . . . ? ' all on an indrawn
    breath.

XLIII *

Mark where the pressing wind shoots javelin-like
Its skeleton shadow on the broad-backed wave !
Here is a fitting spot to dig Love's grave ;
Here where the ponderous breakers plunge and strike,
And dart their hissing tongues high up the sand :
In hearing of the ocean, and in sight
Of those ribbed wind-streaks running into white.
If I the death of Love had deeply planned,
I never could have made it half so sure,
As by the unblest kisses which upbraid
The full-waked sense ; or failing that, degrade !
'Tis morning : but no morning can restore
What we have forfeited. I see no sin :
The wrong is mixed. In tragic life, God wot,
No villain need be ! Passions spin the plot :
We are betrayed by what is false within.

XLIV *

They say, that Pity in Love's service dwells,
A porter at the rosy temple's gate.
I missed him going : but it is my fate
To come upon him now beside his wells ;

Whereby I know that I Love's temple leave,
And that the purple doors have closed behind.
Poor soul ! if, in those early days unkind,
Thy power to sting had been but power to grieve,
We now might with an equal spirit meet,
And not be matched like innocence and vice.
She for the Temple's worship has paid price,
And takes the coin of Pity as a cheat.
She sees through simulation to the bone :
What's best in her impels her to the worst :
Never, she cries, shall Pity soothe Love's thirst,
Or foul hypocrisy for truth atone !

XLV *

It is the season of the sweet wild rose,
My Lady's emblem in the heart of me !
So golden-crownëd shines she gloriously,
And with that softest dream of blood she glows :
Mild as an evening heaven round Hesper bright !
I pluck the flower, and smell it, and revive
The time when in her eyes I stood alive.
I seem to look upon it out of Night.
Here's Madam, stepping hastily. Her whims
Bid her demand the flower, which I let drop.
As I proceed, I feel her sharply stop,
And crush it under heel with trembling limbs.
She joins me in a cat-like way, and talks
Of company, and even condescends
To utter laughing scandal of old friends.
These are the summer days, and these our walks.

XLVI *

At last we parley : we so strangely dumb
In such a close communion ! It befell
About the sounding of the Matin-bell,
And lo ! her place was vacant, and the hum
Of loneliness was round me. Then I rose,
And my disordered brain did guide my foot
To that old wood where our first love-salute
Was interchanged : the source of many throes !

There did I see her, not alone. I moved
Toward her, and made proffer of my arm.
She took it simply, with no rude alarm ;
And that disturbing shadow passed reproved.
I felt the pained speech coming, and declared
My firm belief in her, ere she could speak.
A ghastly morning came into her cheek,
While with a widening soul on me she stared.

XLVII

We saw the swallows gathering in the sky,
And in the osier-isle we heard them noise.
We had not to look back on summer joys,
Or forward to a summer of bright dye :
But in the largeness of the evening earth
Our spirits grew as we went side by side.
The hour became her husband and my bride.
Love, that had robbed us so, thus blessed our dearth !
The pilgrims of the year waxed very loud
In multitudinous chatterings, as the flood
Full brown came from the West, and like pale blood
Expanded to the upper crimson cloud.
Love, that had robbed us of immortal things,
This little moment mercifully gave,
Where I have seen † across the twilight wave
The swan sail with her young beneath her wings.

XLVIII *

Their sense is with their senses all mixed in,
Destroyed by subtleties these women are !
More brain, O Lord, more brain ! or we shall mar
Utterly this fair garden we might win.
Behold ! I looked for peace, and thought it near.
Our inmost hearts had opened, each to each.
We drank the pure daylight of honest speech.
Alas ! that was the fatal draught, I fear.
For when of my lost Lady came the word,
This woman, O this agony of flesh !
Jealous devotion bade her break the mesh,
That I might seek that other like a bird.

† 'And still I see,' in the original version.

I do adore the nobleness ! despise
The act ! She has gone forth, I know not where.
Will the hard world my sentience of her share ?
I feel the truth ; so let the world surmise.

XLIX *

He found her by the ocean's moaning verge,
Nor any wicked change in her discerned ;
And she believed his old love had returned,
Which was her exultation, and her scourge.
She took his hand, and walked with him, and seemed
The wife he sought, though shadow-like and dry.
She had one terror, lest her heart should sigh,
And tell her loudly she no longer dreamed.
She dared not say, ' This is my breast : look in.'
But there's a strength to help the desperate weak.
That night he learned how silence best can speak
The awful things when Pity pleads for Sin.
About the middle of the night her call
Was heard, and he came wondering to the bed.
' Now kiss me, dear ! it may be, now ! ' she said.
Lethe had passed those lips, and he knew all.

L

Thus piteously Love closed what he begat :
The union of this ever-diverse pair !
These two were rapid falcons in a snare,
Condemned to do the flitting of the bat.
Lovers beneath the singing sky of May,
They wandered once ; clear as the dew on flowers :
But they fed not on the advancing hours :
Their hearts held cravings for the buried day.
Then each applied to each that fatal knife,
Deep questioning, which probes to endless dole.
Ah, what a dusty answer gets the soul
When hot for certainties in this our life !—
In tragic hints here see what evermore
Moves dark as yonder midnight ocean's force,
Thundering like ramping hosts of warrior horse,
To throw that faint thin line upon the shore !

THE PATRIOT ENGINEER *

' Sirs ! may I shake your hands ?
　　My countrymen, I see !
I've lived in foreign lands
　　Till England's Heaven to me.
A hearty shake will do me good,
And freshen up my sluggish blood.'

Into his right hand we struck,
Gave the shake, and wish'd him luck.

'—From Austria I come,
　　An English wife to win,
And find an English home,
　　And live and die therein.
Great Lord ! how many a year I've pined
To drink old ale and speak my mind ! '

Loud rang our laughter, and the shout
Hills round the Meuse-boat echoed about.

'—Ay, no offence : laugh on,
　　Young gentlemen : I'll join.
Had you to exile gone,
　　Where free speech is base coin,
You'd sigh to see the jolly nose
Where Freedom's native liquor flows ! '

He this time the laughter led,
Dabbing his oily bullet head.

'—Give me, to suit my moods,
　　An ale-house on a heath,
I'll hand the crags and woods
　　To B'elzebub beneath.
A fig for scenery ! what scene
Can beat a Jackass on a green ? '

The Patriot Engineer

Gravely he seem'd, with gaze intense,
Putting the question to common sense.

> '—Why, there's the ale-house bench :
>   The furze-flower shining round :
> And there's my waiting-wench,
>   As lissome as a hound.
> With " hail Britannia ! " ere I drink,
> I'll kiss her with an artful wink.'

Fair flash'd the foreign landscape while
We breath'd again our native Isle.

> '—The geese may swim hard-by ;
>   They gabble, and you talk :
> You're sure there's not a spy
>   To mark your name with chalk.
> My heart's an oak, and it won't grow
> In flower-pots, foreigners must know.'

Pensive he stood : then shook his head
Sadly ; held out his fist, and said :

> '—You've heard that Hungary's floor'd ?
>   They've got her on the ground.
> A traitor broke her sword :
>   Two despots hold her bound.[1]
> I've seen her gasping her last hope :
> I've seen her sons strung up b' the rope.

> ' Nine gallant gentlemen
>   In Arad they strung up ![2]
> I work'd in peace till then :—
>   That poison'd all my cup.
> A smell of corpses haunted me :
> My nostril sniff'd like life for sea.

> ' Take money for my hire
>   From butchers ?—not the man !
> I've got some natural fire,
>   And don't flash in the pan ;—
> A few ideas I reveal'd :—
> 'Twas well old England stood my shield

     ' Said I, " The Lord of Hosts
       Have mercy on your land !
     I see those dangling ghosts,—
       And you may keep command,
And hang, and shoot, and have your day :
They hold your bill, and you must pay.

     ' " You've sent them where they're strong,
       You carrion Double-Head ! [3]
     I hear them sound a gong
       In Heaven above ! "—I said.
" My God, what feathers won't you moult
For this ! " says I : and then I bolt.

     ' The Bird's a beastly Bird,
       And what is more, a fool.
     I shake hands with the herd
       That flock beneath his rule.
They're kindly ; and their land is fine.
I thought it rarer once than mine.

     ' And rare would be its lot,
       But that he baulks its powers :
     It's just an earthen pot
       For hearts of oak like ours.
Think ! Think !—four days from those frontiers,
And I'm a-head full fifty years.

     ' It tingles to your scalps,
       To think of it, my boys !
     Confusion on their Alps,
       And all their baby toys !
The mountains Britain boasts are men :
And scale you them, my brethren ! '

Cluck, went his tongue ; his fingers, snap.
Britons were proved all heights to cap.

     And we who worshipp'd crags,
       Where purple splendours burn'd,
     Our idol saw in rags,
       And right about were turn'd.
Horizons rich with trembling spires
On violet twilights lost their fires.

And heights where morning wakes
　　With one cheek over snow ;—
And iron-wallèd lakes
　　Where sits the white moon low ;—
For us on youthful travel bent,
The robing picturesque was rent.

Wherever Beauty show'd
　　The wonders of her face,
This man his Jackass rode,
　　High despot of the place.
Fair dreams of our enchanted life
Fled fast from his shrill island fife.

And yet we liked him well ;
　　We laugh'd with honest hearts :—
He shock'd some inner spell,
　　And rous'd discordant parts.
We echoed what we half abjured :
And hating, smilingly endured.

Moreover, could we be
　　To our dear land disloyal ?
And were not also we
　　Of History's blood-Royal ?
We glow'd to think how donkeys graze
In England, thrilling at their brays.

For there a man may view
　　An aspect more sublime
Than Alps against the blue :—
　　The morning eyes of Time !
The very Ass participates
The glory Freedom radiates !

MARIAN

I

SHE can be as wise as we,
　　And wiser when she wishes ;
She can knit with cunning wit,
　　And dress the homely dishes.

She can flourish staff or pen,
    And deal a wound that lingers ;
She can talk the talk of men,
    And touch with thrilling fingers.

II

Match her ye across the sea,
    Natures fond and fiery ;
Ye who zest the turtle's nest
    With the eagle's eyrie.
Soft and loving is her soul,
    Swift and lofty soaring ;
Mixing with its dove-like dole
    Passionate adoring.

III

Such a she who'll match with me ?
    In flying or pursuing,
Subtle wiles are in her smiles
    To set the world a-wooing.
She is steadfast as a star,
    And yet the maddest maiden :
She can wage a gallant war,
    And give the peace of Eden.

ODE TO THE SPIRIT OF EARTH IN AUTUMN

FAIR Mother Earth lay on her back last night,
To gaze her fill on Autumn's sunset skies,
When at a waving of the fallen light
Sprang realms of rosy fruitage o'er her eyes.
A lustrous heavenly orchard hung the West,
Wherein the blood of Eden bloomed again :
Red were the myriad cherub-mouths that pressed,
Among the clusters, rich with song, full fain,
But dumb, because that overmastering spell
Of rapture held them dumb : then, here and there,
A golden harp lost strings ; a crimson shell
Burnt grey ; and sheaves of lustre fell to air.

The illimitable eagerness of hue
Bronzed, and the beamy winged bloom that flew
'Mid those bunched fruits and thronging figures failed.
A green-edged lake of saffron touched the blue,
With isles of fireless purple lying through :
And Fancy on that lake to seek lost treasures sailed.

    Not long the silence followed :
   The voice that issues from thy breast,
      O glorious South-west,
  Along the gloom-horizon holloa'd ;
Warning the valleys with a mellow roar
Through flapping wings ; then sharp the woodland
    bore
   A shudder and a noise of hands :
   A thousand horns from some far vale
   In ambush sounding on the gale.
   Forth from the cloven sky came bands
Of revel-gathering spirits ; trooping down,
Some rode the tree-tops ; some on torn cloud-strips
   Burst screaming thro' the lighted town :
And scudding seaward, some fell on big ships :
    Or mounting the sea-horses blew
   Bright foam-flakes on the black review
   Of heaving hulls and burying beaks.

Still on the farthest line, with outpuffed cheeks,
'Twixt dark and utter dark, the great wind drew
From heaven that disenchanted harmony
To join earth's laughter in the midnight blind :
Booming a distant chorus to the shrieks
              Preluding him : then he,
His mantle streaming thunderingly behind,
Across the yellow realm of stiffened Day,
Shot thro' the woodland alleys signals three ;
   And with the pressure of a sea
Plunged broad upon the vale that under lay.

   Night on the rolling foliage fell :
   But I, who love old hymning night,
   And know the Dryad voices well,
   Discerned them as their leaves took flight,

Like souls to wander after death :
Great armies in imperial dyes,
And mad to tread the air and rise,
The savage freedom of the skies
To taste before they rot. And here,
Like frail white-bodied girls in fear,
The birches swung from shrieks to sighs ;
The aspens, laughers at a breath,
In showering spray-falls mixed their cries,
Or raked a savage ocean-strand
With one incessant drowning screech.
Here stood a solitary beech,
That gave its gold with open hand,
And all its branches, toning chill,
Did seem to shut their teeth right fast,
To shriek more mercilessly shrill,
And match the fierceness of the blast.

But heard I a low swell that noised
Of far-off ocean, I was 'ware
Of pines upon their wide roots poised,
Whom never madness in the air
Can draw to more than loftier stress
Of mournfulness, not mournfulness
For melancholy, but Joy's excess,
That singing on the lap of sorrow faints :
And Peace, as in the hearts of saints
Who chant unto the Lord their God ;
Deep Peace below upon the muffled sod,
The stillness of the sea's unswaying floor.
Could I be sole there not to see
The life within the life awake ;
The spirit bursting from the tree,
And rising from the troubled lake ?
Pour, let the wines of Heaven pour !
The Golden Harp is struck once more,
And all its music is for me !
Pour, let the wines of Heaven pour !
And, ho, for a night of Pagan glee !

There is a curtain o'er us.
For once, good souls, we'll not pretend
To be aught better than her who bore us,
And is our only visible friend.
Hark to her laughter! who laughs like this,
Can she be dead, or rooted in pain?
She has been slain by the narrow brain,
But for us who love her she lives again.
Can she die? O, take her kiss!

The crimson-footed nymph is panting up the glade,
With the wine-jar at her arm-pit, and the drunken ivy-
braid
Round her forehead, breasts, and thighs : starts a
Satyr, and they speed :
Hear the crushing of the leaves : hear the cracking of
the bough!
And the whistling of the bramble, the piping of the
weed!

But the bull-voiced oak is battling now :
The storm has seized him half-asleep,
And round him the wild woodland throngs
To hear the fury of his songs,
The uproar of an outraged deep.
He wakes to find a wrestling giant
Trunk to trunk and limb to limb,
And on his rooted force reliant
He laughs and grasps the broadened giant,
And twist and roll the Anakim ;
And multitudes, acclaiming to the cloud,
Cry which is breaking, which is bowed.

Away, for the cymbals clash aloft
In the circles of pine, on the moss-floor soft.
The nymphs of the woodland are gathering there.
They huddle the leaves, and trample, and toss ;
They swing in the branches, they roll in the moss,
They blow the seed on the air.
Back to back they stand and blow
The winged seed on the cradling air,

D

A fountain of leaves over bosom and back.
The pipe of the Faun comes on their track,
And the weltering alleys overflow
With musical shrieks and wind-wedded hair.
The riotous companies melt to a pair.
    Bless them, mother of kindness !

    A star has nodded through
    The depths of the flying blue.
    Time only to plant the light
    Of a memory in the blindness.
    But time to show me the sight
    Of my life thro' the curtain of night ;
    Shining a moment, and mixed
    With the onward-hurrying stream,
    Whose pressure is darkness to me ;
    Behind the curtain, fixed,
    Beams with endless beam
    That star on the changing sea.

Great Mother Nature ! teach me, like thee,
To kiss the season and shun regrets.
And am I more than the mother who bore,
Mock me not with thy harmony !
    Teach me to blot regrets,
    Great Mother ! me inspire
    With faith that forward sets
    But feeds the living fire,
    Faith that never frets
    For vagueness in the form.
    In life, O keep me warm !
    For, what is human grief ?
    And what do men desire ?
Teach me to feel myself the tree,
    And not the withered leaf.
Fixed am I and await the dark to-be.
    And O, green bounteous Earth !
Bacchante Mother ! stern to those
Who live not in thy heart of mirth ;
Death shall I shrink from, loving thee ?
Into the breast that gives the rose,
    Shall I with shuddering fall ?

Earth, the mother of all,
Moves on her stedfast way,
Gathering, flinging, sowing.
Mortals, we live in her day,
She in her children is growing.

She can lead us, only she,
Unto God's footstool, whither she reaches :
Loved, enjoyed, her gifts must be,
Reverenced the truths she teaches,
Ere a man may hope that he
Ever can attain the glee
Of things without a destiny !

She knows not loss :
She feels but her need,
Who the winged seed
With the leaf doth toss.

And may not men to this attain ?
That the joy of motion, the rapture of being,
Shall throw strong light when our season is
    fleeing,
Nor quicken aged blood in vain,
At the gates of the vault, on the verge of the
    plain ?
Life thoroughly lived is a fact in the brain,
    While eyes are left for seeing.
Behold, in yon stripped Autumn, shivering grey,
    Earth knows no desolation.
    She smells regeneration
    In the moist breath of decay.

Prophetic of the coming joy and strife,
    Like the wild western war-chief sinking
    Calm to the end he eyes unblinking,
Her voice is jubilant in ebbing life.

He for his happy hunting-fields
Forgets the droning chant, and yields
His numbered breaths to exultation
In the proud anticipation :
Shouting the glories of his nation,
Shouting the grandeur of his race,
Shouting his own great deeds of daring :
And when at last death grasps his face,
And stiffened on the ground in peace
He lies with all his painted terrors glaring ;
Hushed are the tribe to hear a threading cry :
Not from the dead man ;
Not from the standers-by :
The spirit of the red man
Is welcomed by his fathers up on high.

LUCIFER IN STARLIGHT *

On a starred night Prince Lucifer uprose.
Tired of his dark dominion swung the fiend
Above the rolling ball in cloud part screened,
Where sinners hugged their spectre of repose.
Poor prey to his hot fit of pride were those.
And now upon his western wing he leaned,
Now his huge bulk o'er Afric's sands careened,
Now the black planet shadowed Arctic snows.
Soaring through wider zones that pricked his scars
With memory of the old revolt from Awe,[1]
He reached a middle height, and at the stars,
Which are the brain of heaven, he looked, and sank.
Around the ancient track marched, rank on rank,
The army of unalterable law.

THE STAR SIRIUS *

Bright Sirius ! that when Orion pales
To dotlings under moonlight still art keen
With cheerful fervour of a warrior's mien
Who holds in his great heart the battle-scales :

Unquenched of flame though swift the flood assails,
Reducing many lustrous to the lean :
Be thou my star, and thou in me be seen
To show what source divine is, and prevails.
Long watches through, at one with godly night,
I mark thee planting joy in constant fire ;
And thy quick beams, whose jets of life inspire
Life to the spirit, passion for the light,
Dark Earth since she first lost her lord [1] from sight
Has viewed and felt them sweep her as a lyre.

EARTH'S SECRET

Not solitarily in fields we find
Earth's secret open, though one page is there ;
Her plainest, such as children spell, and share
With bird and beast ; raised letters for the blind.
Not where the troubled passions toss the mind,
In turbid cities, can the key be bare.
It hangs for those who hither thither fare,
Close interthreading nature with our kind.
They, hearing History speak, of what men were,
And have become, are wise. The gain is great
In vision and solidity ; it lives.
Yet at a thought of life apart from her,
Solidity and vision lose their state,
For Earth, that gives the milk, the spirit gives.

INTERNAL HARMONY

Assured of worthiness we do not dread
Competitors ; we rather give them hail
And greeting in the lists where we may fail :
Must, if we bear an aim beyond the head !
My betters are my masters : purely fed
By their sustainment I likewise shall scale
Some rocky steps between the mount and vale ;
Meanwhile the mark I have and I will wed.

So that I draw the breath of finer air,
Station is nought, nor footways laurel-strewn,
Nor rivals tightly belted for the race.
Good speed to them ! My place is here or there ;
My pride is that among them I have place :
And thus I keep this instrument in tune.

GRACE AND LOVE *

Two flower-enfolding crystal vases she
I love fills daily, mindful but of one :
And close behind pale morn she, like the sun
Priming our world with light, pours, sweet to see,
Clear water in the cup, and into me
The image of herself : and that being done,
Choice of what blooms round her fair garden run
In climbers or in creepers or the tree
She ranges with unerring fingers fine,
To harmony so vivid that through sight
I hear, I have her heavenliness to fold
Beyond the senses, where such love as mine,
Such grace as hers, should the strange Fates withhold
Their starry more from her and me, unite.

THE SPIRIT OF SHAKESPEARE

Thy greatest knew thee, Mother Earth ; unsoured
He knew thy sons. He probed from hell to hell
Of human passions, but of love deflowered
His wisdom was not, for he knew thee well.
Thence came the honeyed corner at his lips,
The conquering smile wherein his spirit sails
Calm as the God who the white sea-wave whips,
Yet full of speech and intershifting tales,

Close mirrors of us : thence had he the laugh
We feel is thine : broad as ten thousand beeves
At pasture ! thence thy songs, that winnow chaff
From grain, bid sick Philosophy's last leaves
Whirl, if they have no response—they enforced
To fatten Earth when from her soul divorced.

APPRECIATION

EARTH was not Earth before her sons appeared,
Nor Beauty Beauty ere young Love was born :
And thou when I lay hidden wast as morn
At city-windows, touching eyelids bleared ;
To none by her fresh wingedness endeared ;
Unwelcome unto revellers outworn.
I the last echoes of Diana's horn
In woodland heard, and saw thee come, and cheered.
No longer wast thou then mere light, fair soul !
And more than simple duty moved thy feet.
New colours rose in thee, from fear, from shame,
From hope, effused : though not less pure a scroll
May men read on the heart I taught to beat :
That change in thee, if not thyself, I claim.

THE WORLD'S ADVANCE *

JUDGE mildly the tasked world ; and disincline
To brand it, for it bears a heavy pack.
You have perchance observed the inebriate's track
At night when he has quitted the inn-sign :
He plays diversions on the homeward line,
Still that way bent albeit his legs are slack :
A hedge may take him, but he turns not back,
Nor turns this burdened world, of curving spine.
' Spiral,' the memorable Lady terms
Our mind's ascent : our world's advance presents
That figure on a flat ; [1] the way of worms.
Cherish the promise of its good intents,
And warn it, not one instinct to efface
Ere Reason ripens for the vacant place.

THE GARDEN OF EPICURUS

THAT Garden of sedate Philosophy
Once flourished, fenced from passion and mishap,
A shining spot upon a shaggy map ;
Where mind and body, in fair junction free,
Luted their joyful concord ; like the tree
From root to flowering twigs a flowing sap.
Clear Wisdom found in tended Nature's lap
Of gentlemen the happy nursery.
That Garden would on light supremest verge,
Were the long drawing of an equal breath
Healthful for Wisdom's head, her heart, her aims.
Our world which for its Babels wants a scourge,
And for its wilds a husbandman, acclaims
The crucifix that came of Nazareth.

A LATER ALEXANDRIAN

[ROSSETTI]

AN inspiration caught from dubious hues
Filled him, and mystic wrynesses he chased ;
For they lead farther than the single-faced,
Wave subtler promise when desire pursues.
The moon of cloud discoloured was his Muse,
His pipe the reed of the old moaning waste.
Love was to him with anguish fast enlaced,
And Beauty where she walked blood-shot the dews.
Men railed at such a singer ; women thrilled
Responsively : he sang not Nature's own
Divinest, but his lyric had a tone,
As 'twere a forest-echo of her voice :
What barrenly they yearn for seemed distilled
From what they dread, who do through tears rejoice.

THE WOODS OF WESTERMAIN *

I

ENTER these enchanted woods,
    You who dare.
Nothing harms beneath the leaves
More than waves a swimmer cleaves.
Toss your heart up with the lark,
Foot at peace with mouse and worm,
    Fair you fare.
Only at a dread of dark
Quaver, and they quit their form :
    Thousand eyeballs under hoods
      Have you by the hair.
Enter these enchanted woods,
    You who dare.

II

Here the snake across your path
Stretches in his golden bath :
Mossy-footed squirrels leap
Soft as winnowing plumes of Sleep :
Yaffles on a chuckle skim
Low to laugh from branches dim :
Up the pine, where sits the star,
Rattles deep the moth-winged jar
Each has business of his own ;
But should you distrust a tone,
    Then beware.
Shudder all the haunted roods,
All the eyeballs under hoods
    Shroud you in their glare.
Enter these enchanted woods,
    You who dare.

III

Open hither, open hence,
Scarce a bramble weaves a fence,
Where the strawberry runs red,
With white star-flower overhead ;

Cumbered by dry twig and cone,
Shredded husks of seedlings flown,
Mine of mole and spotted flint :
Of dire wizardry no hint,
Save mayhap the print that shows
Hasty outward-tripping toes,
Heels to terror, on the mould.
These, the woods of Westermain,
Are as others to behold,
Rich of wreathing sun and rain ;
Foliage lustreful around
Shadowed leagues of slumbering sound.
Wavy tree-tops, yellow whins,
Shelter eager minikins,
Myriads, free to peck and pipe :
Would you better ? would you worse ?
You with them may gather ripe
Pleasures flowing not from purse.
Quick and far as Colour flies
Taking the delighted eyes,
You of any well that springs
May unfold the heaven of things ;
Have it homely and within,
And thereof its likeness win,
Will you so in soul's desire :
This do sages grant t' the lyre.
This is being bird and more,
More than glad musician this ;
Granaries you will have a store
Past the world of woe and bliss ;
Sharing still its bliss and woe ;
Harnessed to its hungers, no.
On the throne Success usurps
You shall seat the joy you feel
Where a race of water chirps,
Twisting hues of flourished steel :
Or where light is caught in hoop
Up a clearing's leafy rise,
Where the crossing deerherds troop
Classic splendours, knightly dyes.
Or, where old-eyed oxen chew

Speculation with the cud,
Read their pool of vision through,
Back to hours when mind was mud ;
Nigh the knot, which did untwine
Timelessly to drowsy suns ;
Seeing Earth a slimy spine,
Heaven a space for winging tons.[1]
Farther, deeper, may you read,
Have you sight for things afield,
Where peeps she, the Nurse of seed,[2]
Cloaked, but in the peep revealed ;
Showing a kind face and sweet :
Look you with the soul you see 't.
Glory narrowing to grace,
Grace to glory magnified,
Following that will you embrace
Close in arms or aëry wide.
Banished is the white Foam-born [3]
Not from here, nor under ban
Phoebus lyrist, Phoebe's horn,
Pipings of the reedy Pan.
Loved of Earth of old they were,
Loving did interpret her ;
And the sterner worship bars
None whom Song has made her stars.
You have seen the huntress moon
Radiantly facing dawn,
Dusky meads between them strewn
Glimmering like downy awn :
Argent Westward glows the hunt,
East the blush about to climb ;
One another fair they front,
Transient, yet outshine the time ;
Even as dewlight off the rose
In the mind a jewel sows.
Thus opposing grandeurs live
Here if Beauty be their dower :
Doth she of her spirit give,
Fleetingness will spare her flower.
This is in the tune we play,
Which no spring of strength would quell ;

In subduing does not slay ;
Guides the channel, guards the well :
Tempered holds the young blood-heat,
Yet through measured grave accord
Hears the heart of wildness beat
Like a centaur's hoof on sward.
Drink the sense the notes infuse,
You a larger self will find :
Sweetest fellowship ensues
With the creatures of your kind.
Ay, and Love, if Love it be
Flaming over *I* and *ME*,
Love meet they who do not shove
Cravings in the van of Love.
Courtly dames are here to woo,
Knowing love if it be true.
Reverence the blossom-shoot
Fervently, they are the fruit.
Mark them stepping, hear them talk,
Goddess is no myth inane,
You will say of those who walk
In the woods of Westermain.
Waters that from throat and thigh
Dart the sun his arrows back ;
Leaves that on a woodland sigh
Chat of secret things no lack ;
Shadowy branch-leaves, waters clear,
Bare or veiled they move sincere ;
Not by slavish terrors tripped ;
Being anew in nature dipped,
Growths of what they step on, these ;
With the roots the grace of trees.
Casket-breasts they give, nor hide,
For a tyrant's flattered pride,
Mind, which nourished not by light,
Lurks the shuffling trickster sprite : [4]
Whereof are strange tales to tell ;
Some in blood writ, tombed in hell.
Here the ancient battle ends,
Joining two astonished friends,
Who the kiss can give and take

With more warmth than in that world
Where the tiger claws the snake,
Snake her tiger clasps infurled,
And the issue of their fight
Peoples lands in snarling plight.
Here her splendid beast she leads
Silken-leashed and decked with weeds
Wild as he, but breathing faint
Sweetness of unfelt constraint.
Love, the great volcano, flings
Fires of lower Earth to sky ;
Love, the sole permitted, sings
Sovereignly of *ME* and *I*.
Bowers he has of sacred shade,
Spaces of superb parade,
Voiceful. . . . But bring you a note
Wrangling, howsoe'er remote,
Discords out of discord spin
Round and round derisive din :
Sudden will a pallor pant
Chill at screeches miscreant ;
Owls or spectres, thick they flee ;
Nightmare upon horror broods ;
Hooded laughter, monkish glee,
 Gaps the vital air.
Enter these enchanted woods
 You who dare.

IV

You must love the light so well
That no darkness will seem fell.
Love it so you could accost
Fellowly a livid ghost.
Whish ! the phantom wisps away,
Owns him smoke to cocks of day.
In your breast the light must burn
Fed of you, like corn in quern
Ever plumping while the wheel
Speeds the mill and drains the meal.

Light to light sees little strange,
Only features heavenly new ;
Then you touch the nerve of Change,
Then of Earth you have the clue ;
Then her two-sexed meanings melt
Through you, wed the thought and felt.
Sameness locks no scurfy pond
Here for Custom, crazy-fond :
Change is on the wing to bud
Rose in brain from rose in blood.
Wisdom throbbing shall you see
Central in complexity ;
From her pasture 'mid the beasts
Rise to her ethereal feasts,
Not, though lightnings track your wit
Starward, scorning them you quit :
For be sure the bravest wing
Preens it in our common spring,
Thence along the vault to soar,
You with others, gathering more,
Glad of more, till you reject
Your proud title of elect,
Perilous even here while few
Roam the arched greenwood with you.
    Heed that snare.
Muffled by his cavern-cowl
Squats the scaly Dragon-fowl,[5]
Who was lord ere light you drank,
And lest blood of knightly rank
Stream, let not your fair princess
Stray : he holds the leagues in stress,
    Watches keenly there.
Oft has he been riven ; slain
Is no force in Westermain.
Wait, and we shall forge him curbs,
Put his fangs to uses, tame,
Teach him, quick as cunning herbs,
How to cure him sick and lame.
Much restricted, much enringed,
Much he frets, the hooked and winged,
    Never known to spare.

'Tis enough : the name of Sage
Hits no thing in nature, nought ;
Man the least, save when grave Age
From yon Dragon guards his thought.
Eye him when you hearken dumb
To what words from Wisdom come.
When she says how few are by
Listening to her, eye his eye.
      Self, his name declare.
Him shall Change, transforming late,
Wonderously renovate.
Hug himself the creature may :
What he hugs is loathed decay.
Crying, slip thy scales, and slough !
Change will strip his armour off ;
Make of him who was all maw,
Inly only thrilling-shrewd,
Such a servant as none saw
Through his days of dragonhood :
Days when growling o'er his bone,
Sharpened he for mine and thine ;
Sensitive within alone ;
Scaly as in clefts of pine.
Change, the strongest son of Life,
Has the Spirit here to wife.
Lo, their young of vivid breed
Bear the lights that onward speed,
Threading thickets, mounting glades,
Up the verdurous colonnades,
Round the fluttered curves, and down,
Out of sight of Earth's blue crown,
Whither, in her central space,
Spouts the Fount and Lure o' the chase.[6]
Fount unresting, Lure divine !
There meet all : too late look most.
Fire in water hued as wine
Springs amid a shadowy host ;
Circled : one close-headed mob,
Breathless, scanning divers heaps
Where a Heart begins to throb,
Where it ceases, slow, with leaps :

And 'tis very strange, 'tis said,
How you spy in each of them
Semblance of that Dragon red,
As the oak in bracken-stem.[7]
And, 'tis said, how each and each :
Which commences, which subsides :
First my Dragon ! doth beseech
Her who food for all provides.[8]
And she answers with no sign ;
Utters neither yea nor nay ;
Fires the water hued as wine ;
Kneads another spark in clay.
Terror is about her hid ;
Silence of the thunders locked ;
Lightnings lining the shut lid ;
Fixity on quaking rocked.
Lo, you look at Flow and Drought
Interflashed and interwrought :
Ended is begun, begun
Ended, quick as torrents run.
Young Impulsion spouts to sink ;
Luridness and lustre link ;
'Tis your come and go of breath ;
Mirrored pants the Life, the Death ;
Each of either reaped and sown :
Rosiest rosy wanes to crone.
See you so ? your senses drift ;
'Tis a shuttle weaving swift.
Look with spirit past the sense,
Spirit shines in permanence.
That is She, the view of whom
Is the dust within the tomb,
Is the inner blush above,
Look to loathe, or look to love ;
Think her Lump, or know her Flame ;
Dread her scourge, or read her aim ;
Shoot your hungers from their nerve ;
Or, in her example, serve.
Some have found her sitting grave ;
Laughing, some ; or, browed with sweat,
Hurling dust of fool and knave

In a hissing smithy's jet.
More it were not well to speak ;
Burn to see, you need but seek.
Once beheld she gives the key
Airing every doorway, she ;
Little can you stop or steer
Ere of her you are the seër,
On the surface she will witch,
Rendering Beauty yours, but gaze
Under, and the soul is rich
Past computing, past amaze.
Then is courage that endures
Even her awful tremble yours.
Then, the reflex of that Fount
Spied below, will Reason mount
Lordly and a quenchless force,
Lighting Pain to its mad source,
Scaring Fear till Fear escapes,
Shot through all its phantom shapes.
Then your spirit will perceive
Fleshly seed of fleshly sins ;
Where the passions interweave,
How the serpent tangle spins
Of the sense of Earth misprised,
Brainlessly unrecognized ;
She being Spirit in her clods
Footway to the God of Gods.
Then for you are pleasures pure,
Sureties as the stars are sure :
Not the wanton beckoning flags
Which, of flattery and delight,
Wax to the grim Habit-Hags
Riding souls of men to night :
Pleasures that through blood run sane,
Quickening spirit from the brain,
Each of each in sequent birth,
Blood and brain and spirit, three
(Say the deepest gnomes of Earth),
Join for true felicity.
Are they parted, then expect
Some one sailing will be wrecked :

E

Separate hunting are they sped,
Scan the morsel coveted.
Earth that Triad is : [9] she hides
Joy from him who that divides ;
Showers it when the three are one
Glassing her in union.
Earth your haven, Earth your helm,
You command a double realm ;
Labouring here to pay your debt,
Till your little sun shall set ;
Leaving her the future task :
Loving her too well to ask.
Eglantine that climbs the yew,
She her darkest wreathes for those
Knowing her the Ever-new,
And themselves the kin o' the rose.
Life, the chisel, axe and sword,
Wield who have her depths explored : [10]
Life, the dream, shall be their robe,
Large as air about the globe ;
Life, the question, hear its cry
Echoed with concordant Why ;
Life, the small self-dragon ramped,
Thrill for service to be stamped.
Ay, and over every height
Life for them shall wave a wand :
That, the last, where sits affright,
Homely shows the stream beyond.
Love the light and be its lynx,
You will track her and attain ;
Read her as no cruel Sphinx
In the woods of Westermain.
Daily fresh the woods are ranged ;
Glooms which otherwhere appal,
Sounded : here, their worths exchanged,
Urban joins with pastoral :
Little lost, save what may drop
Husk-like, and the mind preserves.
Natural overgrowths they lop,
Yet from nature neither swerves,
Trained or savage : for this cause :

Of our Earth they ply the laws,
Have in Earth their feeding root,
Mind of man and bent of brute.
Hear that song ; both wild and ruled.
Hear it : is it wail or mirth ?
Ordered, bubbled, quite unschooled ?
None, and all : it springs of Earth.
O but hear it ! 'tis the mind ;
Mind that with deep Earth unites,
Round the solid trunk to wind
Rings of clasping parasites.
Music have you there to feed
Simplest and most soaring need.
Free to wind, and in desire
Winding, they to her attached
Feel the trunk a spring of fire,
And ascend to heights unmatched,
Whence the tidal world is viewed
As a sea of windy wheat,
Momently black, barren, rude ;
Golden-brown, for harvest meet ;
Dragon-reaped from folly-sown ;
Bride-like to the sickle-blade :
Quick it varies, while the moan,
Moan of a sad creature strayed,
Chiefly is its voice. So flesh
Conjures tempest-flails to thresh
Good from worthless. Some clear lamps
Light it ; more of dead marsh-damps.
Monster is it still, and blind,
Fit but to be led by Pain.
Glance we at the paths behind,
Fruitful sight has Westermain.
There we laboured, and in turn
Forward our blown lamps discern,
As you see on the dark deep
Far the loftier billows leap,
 Foam for beacon bear.
Hither, hither, if you will,
Drink instruction, or instil,
Run the woods like vernal sap,

Crying, hail to luminousness !
    But have care.
In yourself may lurk the trap :
On conditions they caress.
Here you meet the light invoked :
Here is never secret cloaked.
Doubt you with the monster's fry
All his orbit may exclude ;
Are you of the stiff, the dry,
Cursing the not understood ;
Grasp you with the monster's claws ;
Govern with his truncheon-saws ;
Hate, the shadow of a grain ;
You are lost in Westermain ; [11]
Earthward swoops a vulture sun,
Nighted upon carrion :
Straightway venom winecups shout
Toasts to One whose eyes are out : [12]
Flowers along the reeling floor
Drip henbane and hellebore :
Beauty, of her tresses shorn,
Shrieks as nature's maniac :
Hideousness on hoof and horn
Tumbles, yapping in her track :
Haggard Wisdom, stately once,
Leers fantastical and trips : .
Allegory drums the sconce,
Impiousness nibblenips.
Imp that dances, imp that flits,
Imp o' the demon-growing girl,
Maddest ! whirl with imp o' the pits
Round you, and with them you whirl
Fast where pours the fountain-rout
Out of Him whose eyes are out :
Multitudes on multitudes,
Drenched in wallowing devilry :
And you ask where you may be,
    In what reek of a lair
Given to bones and ogre-broods :
    And they yell you Where.
Enter these enchanted woods,
    You who dare.

A BALLAD OF PAST MERIDIAN

I

Last night returning from my twilight walk
I met the grey mist Death, whose eyeless brow
Was bent on me, and from his hand of chalk
He reached me flowers as from a withered bough :
O Death, what bitter nosegays givest thou !

II

Death said, I gather, and pursued his way.
Another stood by me, a shape in stone,
Sword-hacked and iron-stained, with breasts of clay,
And metal veins that sometimes fiery shone :
O Life, how naked and how hard when known !

III

Life said, As thou hast carved me, such am I.
Then memory, like the nightjar on the pine,
And sightless hope, a woodlark in night sky,
Joined notes of Death and Life till night's decline :
Of Death, of Life, those inwound notes are mine.

THE DAY OF THE DAUGHTER OF HADES *

I

He who has looked upon Earth
Deeper than flower and fruit,
Losing some hue of his mirth,
As the tree striking rock at the root,
Unto him shall the marvellous tale
Of Callistes more humanly come
With the touch on his breast than a hail
From the markets that hum.

II

Now the youth footed swift to the dawn.
'Twas the season when wintertide,
In the higher rock-hollows updrawn,
Leaves meadows to bud, and he spied,
By light throwing shallow shade,
Between the beam and the gloom,
Sicilian Enna, whose Maid
Such aspect wears in her bloom
Underneath since the Charioteer
Of Darkness whirled her away,
On a reaped afternoon of the year,
Nigh the poppy-droop of Day.
O and naked of her, all dust,
The majestic Mother and Nurse,
Ringing cries to the God, the Just,
Curled the land with the blight of her curse :
Recollected of this glad isle
Still quaking. But now more fair,
And momently fraying the while
The veil of the shadows there,
Soft Enna that prostrate grief
Sang through, and revealed round the vines,
Bronze-orange, the crisp young leaf,
The wheat-blades tripping in lines,
A hue unillumined by sun
Of the flowers flooding grass as from founts :
All the penetrable dun
      Of the morn ere she mounts.

III

Nor had saffron and sapphire and red
Waved aloft to their sisters below,
When gaped by the rock-channel head
Of the lake, black, a cave at one blow,
Reverberant over the plain :
A sound oft fearfully swung
For the coming of wrathful rain :
And forth, like the dragon-tongue
Of a fire beaten flat by the gale,

But more as the smoke to behold,
A chariot burst. Then a wail
Quivered high of the love that would fold
Bliss immeasurable, bigger than heart,
Though a God's : and the wheels were stayed,
And the team of the chariot swart
Reared in marble, the six, dismayed,
Like hoofs that by night plashing sea
Curve and ramp from the vast swan-wave :
For, lo, the Great Mother, She !
And Callistes gazed, he gave
His eyeballs up to the sight :
The embrace of the Twain, of whom
To men are their day, their night,
Mellow fruits and the shearing tomb :
Our Lady of the Sheaves
And the Lily of Hades, the Sweet
Of Enna : he saw through leaves
The Mother and Daughter meet.
They stood by the chariot-wheel,
Embraced, very tall, most like
Fellow poplars, wind-taken, that reel
Down their shivering columns and strike
Head to head, crossing throats : and apart,
For the feast of the look, they drew,
Which Darkness no longer could thwart ;
And they broke together anew,
Exulting to tears, flower and bud.
But the mate of the Rayless was grave :
She smiled like Sleep on its flood,
That washes of all we crave :
Like the trance of eyes awake
And the spirit enshrouded, she cast
The wan underworld on the lake.
    They were so, and they passed.

                    IV

He tells it, who knew the law
Upon mortals : he stood alive
Declaring that this he saw :
    He could see, and survive.

V

Now the youth was not ware of the beams
With the grasses intertwined,
For each thing seen, as in dreams,
Came stepping to rear through his mind,
Till it struck his remembered prayer
To be witness of this which had flown
Like a smoke melted thinner than air,
That the vacancy doth disown.
And viewing a maiden, he thought
It might now be morn, and afar
Within him the memory wrought
Of a something that slipped from the car
When those, the august, moved by :
Perchance a scarf, and perchance
This maiden. She did not fly,
Nor started at his advance :
She looked, as when infinite thirst
Pants pausing to bless the springs,
Refreshed, unsated. Then first
He trembled with awe of the things
He had seen ; and he did transfer,
Divining and doubting in turn,
His reverence unto her ;
Nor asked what he crouched to learn :
The whence of her, whither, and why
Her presence there, and her name,
Her parentage : under which sky
Her birth, and how hither she came,
So young, a virgin, alone,
Unfriended, having no fear,
As Oreads have ; no moan,
Like the lost upon earth ; no tear ;
Not a sign of the torch in the blood,
Though her stature had reached the height
When mantles a tender rud
In maids that of youths have sight,
If maids of our seed they be :
For he said : A glad vision art thou !
And she answered him : Thou to me !
    As men utter a vow.

VI

Then said she, quick as the cries
Of the rainy cranes : Light ! light !
And Helios rose in her eyes,
That were full as the dew-balls bright,
Relucent to him as dews
Unshaded. Breathing, she sent
Her voice to the God of the Muse,
And along the vale it went,
Strange to hear : not thin, not shrill :
Sweet, but no young maid's throat :
The echo beyond the hill
Ran falling on half the note :
And under the shaken ground
Where the Hundred-headed groans
By the roots of great Aetna bound,
As of him were hollow tones
Of wondering roared : a tale
Repeated to sunless halls.
But now off the face of the vale
Shadows fled in a breath, and the walls
Of the lake's rock-head were gold,
And the breast of the lake, that swell
Of the crestless long wave rolled
To shore-bubble, pebble and shell.
A morning of radiant lids
O'er the dance of the earth opened wide :
The bees chose their flowers, the snub kids
Upon hindlegs went sportive, or plied,
Nosing, hard at the dugs to be filled :
There was milk, honey, music to make :
Up their branches the little birds billed :
Chirrup, drone, bleat and buzz ringed the lake.
O shining in sunlight, chief
After water and water's caress,
Was the young bronze-orange leaf,
That clung to the tree as a tress,
Shooting lucid tendrils to wed
With the vine-hook tree or pole,
Like Arachne launched out on her thread.

Then the maiden her dusky stole
In the span of the black-starred zone
Gathered up for her footing fleet.
As one that had toil of her own
She followed the lines of wheat
Tripping straight through the field, green blades,
To the groves of olive grey,
Downy-grey, golden-tinged : and to glades
Where the pear-blossom thickens the spray
In a night, like the snow-packed storm :
Pear, apple, almond, plum :
Not wintry now : pushing, warm !
And she touched them with finger and thumb,
As the vine-hook closes : she smiled,
Recounting again and again,
Corn, wine, fruit, oil ! like a child,
With the meaning known to men.
For hours in the track of the plough
And the pruning-knife she stepped,
And of how the seed works, and of how
Yields the soil, she seemed adept.
Then she murmured that name of the dearth,
The Beneficent, Hers, who bade
Our husbandmen sow for the birth
Of the grain making earth full glad.
She murmured that Other's : the dirge
Of life-light: for whose dark lap
Our locks are clipped on the verge
Of the realm where runs no sap.[1]
She said : We have looked on both !
And her eyes had a wavering beam
Of various lights, like the froth
Of the storm-swollen ravine stream
In flame of the bolt. What links
Were these which had made him her friend ?
He eyed her, as one who drinks,
    And would drink to the end.

VII

Now the meadows with crocus besprent,
And the asphodel woodsides she left,

And the lake-slopes, the ravishing scent
Of narcissus, dark-sweet, for the cleft
That tutors the torrent-brook,
Delaying its forceful spleen
With many a wind and crook
Through rock to the broad ravine.
By the hyacinth-bells in the brakes,
And the shade-loved white windflower, half hid,
And the sun-loving lizards and snakes
On the cleft's barren ledges, that slid
Out of sight, smooth as waterdrops, all,
At a snap of twig or bark
In the track of the foreign foot-fall,
She climbed to the pineforest dark,
Overbrowing an emerald chine
Of the grass-billows. Thence, as a wreath,
Running poplar and cypress to pine,
The lake-banks are seen, and beneath,
Vineyard, village, groves, rivers, towers, farms,
The citadel watching the bay,
The bay with the town in its arms,
The town shining white as the spray
Of the sapphire sea-wave on the rock,
Where the rock stars the girdle of sea,
White-ringed, as the midday flock,
Clipped by heat, rings the round of the tree.
That hour of the piercing shaft
Transfixes bough-shadows, confused
In veins of fire, and she laughed,
With her quiet mouth amused,
To see the whole flock, adroop,
Asleep, hug the tree-stem as one,
Imperceptibly filling the loop
Of its shade at a slant of sun.
The pipes under pent of the crag,
Where the goatherds in piping recline,
Have whimsical stops, burst and flag
Uncorrected as outstretched swine :
For the fingers are slack and unsure,
And the wind issues querulous :—thorns
And snakes !—but she listened demure,

Comparing day's music with morn's.
Of the gentle spirit that slips
From the bark of the tree she discoursed,
And of her of the wells, whose lips
Are coolness enchanting, rock-sourced.
And much of the sacred loon,
The frolic, the Goatfoot God,
For stories of indolent noon
In the pineforest's odorous nod,
She questioned, not knowing : he can
Be waspish, irascible, rude,
He is oftener friendly to man,
And ever to beasts and their brood.
For the which did she love him well,
She said, and his pipes of the reed,
His twitched lips puffing to tell
In music his tears and his need,
Against the sharp catch of his hurt.
Not as shepherds of Pan did she speak,
Nor spake as the schools, to divert,
But fondly, perceiving him weak
Before Gods, and to shepherds a fear,
A holiness, horn and heel.
All this she had learnt in her ear
From Callistes, and taught him to feel.
Yea, the solemn divinity flushed
Through the shaggy brown skin of the beast,
And the steeps where the cataract rushed,
And the wilds where the forest is priest,
Were his temple to clothe him in awe,
While she spake : 'twas a wonder : she read
The haunts of the beak and the claw
As plain as the land of bread,
But Cities and martial States,
Whither soon the youth veered his theme,
Were impervious barrier-gates
To her : and that ship, a trireme,
Nearing harbour, scarce wakened her glance,
Though he dwelt on the message it bore
Of sceptre and sword and lance
To the bee-swarms black on the shore,

Which were audible almost,
So black they were. It befell
That he called up the warrior host
Of the Song pouring hydromel
In thunder, the wide-winged Song.
And he named with his boyish pride
The heroes, the noble throng
Past Acheron now, foul tide !
With his joy of the godlike band
And the verse divine, he named
The chiefs pressing hot on the strand,
Seen of Gods, of Gods aided, and maimed.
The fleetfoot and ireful ; the King ;
Him, the prompter in stratagem,
Many-shifted and masterful : Sing,
O Muse ! But she cried : Not of them !
She breathed as if breath had failed,
And her eyes, while she bade him desist,
Held the lost-to-light ghosts grey-mailed,
As you see the grey-river mist
Hold shapes on the yonder bank.
A moment her body waned,
The light of her sprang and sank :
Then she looked at the sun, she regained
Clear feature, and she breathed deep.
She wore the wan smile he had seen,
As the flow of the river of Sleep,
On the mouth of the Shadow-Queen.
In sunlight she craved to bask,
Saying : Life ! And who was she ? who ?
Of what issue ? He dared not ask,
    For that partly he knew.

VIII

A noise of the hollow ground
Turned the eye to the ear in debate :
Not the soft overflowing of sound
Of the pines, ranked, lofty, straight,
Barely swayed to some whispers remote,
Some swarming whispers above :
Not the pines with the faint airs afloat,

Hush-hushing the nested dove :
It was not the pines, or the rout
Oft heard from mid-forest in chase,
But the long muffled roar of a shout
Subterranean. Sharp grew her face.
She rose, yet not moved by affright ;
'Twas rather good haste to use
Her holiday of delight
In the beams of the God of the Muse.
And the steeps of the forest she crossed,
On its dry red sheddings and cones
Up the paths by roots green-mossed,
Spotted amber, and old mossed stones.
Then out where the brook-torrents starts
To her leap, and from bend to curve
A hurrying elbow darts
For the instant-glancing swerve,
Decisive, with violent will
In the action formed, like hers,
The maiden's, ascending ; and still
Ascending, the bud of the furze,
The broom, and all blue-berried shoots
Of stubborn and prickly kind,
The juniper flat on its roots,
The dwarf rhododaphne, behind
She left, and the mountain sheep
Far behind, goat, herbage and flower.
The island was hers, and the deep,
All heaven, a golden hour.
Then with wonderful voice that rang
Through air as the swan's nigh death,
Of the glory of Light she sang,
She sang of the rapture of Breath.
Nor ever, says he who heard,
Heard Earth in her boundaries broad,
From bosom of singer or bird
A sweetness thus rich of the God
Whose harmonies always are sane.
She sang of furrow and seed,
The burial, birth of the grain,
The growth, and the showers that feed,

And the green blades waxing mature
For the husbandman's armful brown.
O, the song in its burden ran pure,
And burden to song was a crown.
Callistes, a singer, skilled
In the gift he could measure and praise,
By a rival's art was thrilled,
Though she sang but a Song of Days,
Where the husbandman's toil and strife
Little varies to strife and toil :
But the milky kernel of life,
With her numbered : corn, wine, fruit, oil !
The song did give him to eat :
Gave the first rapt vision of Good,
And the fresh young sense of Sweet :
The grace of the battle for food,
With the issue Earth cannot refuse
When men to their labour are sworn.
'Twas a song of the God of the Muse
    To the forehead of Morn.

IX

Him loved she. Lo, now was he veiled :
Over sea stood a swelled cloud-rack :
The fishing-boat havenward sailed,
Bent abeam with a whitened track,
Surprised, fast hauling the net,
As it flew : sea dashed, earth shook.
She said : Is it night ? O not yet !
With a travail of thoughts in her look.
The mountain heaved up to its peak :
Sea darkened : earth gathered her fowl :
Of bird or of branch rose the shriek.
Night ? but never so fell a scowl
Wore night, nor the sky since then
When ocean ran swallowing shore,
And the Gods looked down for men.
Broke tempest with that stern roar
Never yet, save when black on the whirl
Rode wrath of a sovereign Power.
Then the youth and the shuddering girl,

Dim as shades in the angry shower,
Joined hands and descended a maze
Of the paths that were racing alive
Round boulder and bush, cleaving ways,
Incessant, with sound of a hive.
The height was a fountain-urn
Pouring streams, and the whole solid height
Leaped, chasing at every turn
The pair in one spirit of flight
To the folding pineforest. Yet here,
Like the pause to things hunted, in doubt,
The stillness bred spectral fear
Of the awfulness ranging without,
And imminent. Downward they fled,
From under the haunted roof,
To the valley aquake with the tread
Of an iron-resounding hoof,
As of legions of thunderful horse
Broken loose and in line tramping hard.
For the rage of a hungry force
Roamed blind of its mark over sward :
They saw it rush dense in the cloak
Of its travelling swathe of steam,
All the vale through a thin thread-smoke
Was thrown back to distance extreme :
And dull the full breast of it blinked,
Like a buckler of steel breathed o'er,
Diminished, in strangeness distinct,
Glowing cold, unearthly, hoar :
An Enna of fields beyond sun,
Out of light, in a lurid web,
And the traversing fury spun
Up and down with a wave's flow and ebb ;
As the wave breaks to grasp and to spurn,
Retire, and in ravenous greed,
Inveterate, swell its return.
Up and down, as if wringing from speed
Sights that made the unsighted appear,
Delude and dissolve, on it scoured.
Lo, a sea upon land held career
Through the plain of the vale half-devoured.

Callistes of home and escape
Muttered swiftly, unwitting of speech.
She gazed at the Void of shape,
She put her white hand to his reach,
Saying : Now have we looked on the Three.[2]
And divided from day, from night,
From air that is breath, stood she,
    Like the vale, out of light.

x

Then again in disorderly words
He muttered of home, and was mute,
With the heart of the cowering birds
Ere they burst off the fowler's foot.
He gave her some redness that streamed
Through her limbs in a flitting glow.
The sigh of our life she seemed,
The bliss of it clothing in woe.
Frailer than flower when the round
Of the sickle encircles it : strong
To tell of the things profound,
Our inmost uttering song
Unspoken. So stood she awhile
In the gloom of the terror afield,
And the silence about her smile
Said more than of tongue is revealed.
I have breathed : I have gazed : I have been :
It said : and not joylessly shone
The remembrance of light through the screen
Of a face that seemed shadow and stone.
She led the youth trembling, appalled,
To the lake-banks he saw sink and rise
Like a panic-struck breast. Then she called,
And the hurricane blackness had eyes.
It launched like the Thunderer's bolt.
Pale she drooped, and the youth by her side
Would have clasped her and dared a revolt
Sacrilegious as ever defied
High Olympus, but vainly for strength
His compassionate heart shook a frame

F

Stricken rigid to ice all its length.
On amain the black traveller came.
Lo, a chariot, cleaving the storm,
Clove the fountaining lake with a plough,
And the lord of the steeds was in form
He, the God of implacable brow,
Darkness : he : he in person : he raged
Through the wave like a boar of the wilds
From the hunters and hounds disengaged,
And a name shouted hoarsely : his child's.
Horror melted in anguish to hear.
Lo, the wave hissed apart for the path
Of the terrible Charioteer,
With the foam and torn features of wrath,
Hurled aloft on each arm in a sheet ;
And the steeds clove it, rushing at land
Like the teeth of the famished at meat.
        Then he swept out his hand.

                    XI

This, no more, doth Callistes recall :
He saw, ere he dropped in swoon,
On the maiden the chariot fall,
As a thundercloud swings on the moon.
Forth, free of the deluge, one cry
From the vanishing gallop rose clear :
And : Skiágeneia ! the sky
Rang : Skiágeneia ! the sphere.
And she left him therewith, to rejoice,
Repine, yearn, and know not his aim,
The life of their day in her voice,
        Left her life in her name.

                    XII

Now the valley in ruin of fields
And fair meadowland, showing at eve
Like the spear-pitted warrior's shields
After battle, bade men believe
That no other than wrathfullest God

Had been loose on her beautiful breast,
Where the flowery grass was clod,
Wheat and vine as a trailing nest.
The valley, discreet in grief,
Disclosed but the open truth,
And Enna had hope of the sheaf :
There was none for the desolate youth
Devoted to mourn and to crave.
Of the secret he had divined
Of his friend of a day would he rave :
How for light of our earth she pined :
For the olive, the vine and the wheat
Burning through with inherited fire :
And when Mother went Mother to meet,
She was prompted by simple desire
In the day-destined car to have place
At the skirts of the Goddess, unseen,
And be drawn to the dear earth's face.
She was fire for the blue and the green
Of our earth, dark fire ; athirst
As a seed of her bosom for dawn,
White air that had robed and nursed
Her mother. Now was she gone
With the Silent, the God without tear,
Like a bud peeping out of its sheath
To be sundered and stamped with the sere.
And Callistes to her beneath,
As she to our beams, extinct,
Strained arms : he was shade of her shade.
In division so were they linked.
But the song which had betrayed
Her flight to the cavernous ear
For its own keenly wakeful : that song
Of the sowing and reaping, and cheer
Of the husbandman's heart made strong
Through droughts and deluging rains
With his faith in the Great Mother's love :
O the joy of the breath she sustains,
And the lyre of the light above,
And the first rapt vision of Good,
And the fresh young sense of Sweet :

That song the youth ever pursued
In the track of her footing fleet.
For men to be profited much
By her day upon earth did he sing :
Of her voice, and her steps, and her touch
On the blossoms of tender Spring,
Immortal : and how in her soul
She is with them, and tearless abides,
Folding grain of a love for one goal
In patience, past flowing of tides.
And if unto him she was tears,
He wept not : he wasted within :
Seeming sane in the song, to his peers,
Only crazed where the cravings begin.
Our Lady of Gifts prized he less
Than her issue in darkness : the dim
Lost Skiágeneia's caress
Of our earth made it richest for him.
And for that was a curse on him raised,
And he withered rathe, dry to his prime,
Though the bounteous Giver he praised
Through the island with rites of old time
Exceedingly fervent, and reaped
Veneration for teachings devout,
Pious hymns when the corn-sheaves are heaped,
And the wine-presses ruddily spout,
And the olive and apple are juice
At a touch light as hers lost below.
Whatsoever to men is of use
Sprang his worship of them who bestow,
In a measure of songs unexcelled :
But that soul loving earth and the sun
From her home of the shadows he held
For his beacon where beam there is none :
And to join her, or have her brought back,
In his frenzy the singer would call,
Till he followed where never was track,
    On the path trod of all.

THE LARK ASCENDING

He rises and begins to round,
He drops the silver chain of sound,
Of many links without a break,
In chirrup, whistle, slur and shake,
All intervolved and spreading wide,
Like water-dimples down a tide
Where ripple ripple overcurls
And eddy into eddy whirls ;
A press of hurried notes that run
So fleet they scarce are more than one,
Yet changeingly the trills repeat
And linger ringing while they fleet,
Sweet to the quick o' the ear, and dear
To her beyond the handmaid ear,
Who sits beside our inner springs,
Too often dry for this he brings,
Which seems the very jet of earth
At sight of sun, her music's mirth,
As up he wings the spiral stair,
A song of light, and pierces air
With fountain ardour, fountain play,
To reach the shining tops of day,
And drink in everything discerned
An ecstasy to music turned,
Impelled by what his happy bill
Disperses ; drinking, showering still,
Unthinking save that he may give
His voice the outlet, there to live
Renewed in endless notes of glee,
So thirsty of his voice is he,
For all to hear and all to know
That he is joy, awake, aglow,
The tumult of the heart to hear
Through pureness filtered crystal-clear,
And know the pleasure sprinkled bright
By simple singing of delight,
Shrill, irreflective, unrestrained,
Rapt, ringing, on the jet sustained

Without a break, without a fall,
Sweet-silvery, sheer lyrical,
Perennial, quavering up the chord
Like myriad dews of sunny sward
That trembling into fulness shine,
And sparkle dropping argentine ;
Such wooing as the ear receives
From zephyr caught in choric leaves
Of aspens when their chattering net
Is flushed to white with shivers wet ;
And such the water-spirit's chime
On mountain heights in morning's prime,
Too freshly sweet to seem excess,
Too animate to need a stress ;
But wider over many heads.
The starry voice ascending spreads,
Awakening, as it waxes thin,
The best in us to him akin ;
And every face to watch him raised
Puts on the light of children praised,
So rich our human pleasure ripes
When sweetness on sincereness pipes,
Though nought be promised from the seas,
But only a soft-ruffling breeze
Sweep glittering on a still content,
Serenity in ravishment.

For singing till his heaven fills,
'Tis love of earth that he instils,
And ever winging up and up,
Our valley is his golden cup,
And he the wine which overflows
To lift us with him as he goes :
The woods and brooks, the sheep and kine,
He is, the hills, the human line,
The meadows green, the fallows brown,
The dreams of labour in the town ;
He sings the sap, the quickened veins ;
The wedding song of sun and rains
He is, the dance of children, thanks
Of sowers, shout of primrose-banks,

And eye of violets while they breathe ;
All these the circling song will wreathe,
And you shall hear the herb and tree,
The better heart of men shall see,
Shall feel celestially, as long
As you crave nothing save the song.

Was never voice of ours could say
Our inmost in the sweetest way,
Like yonder voice aloft, and link
All hearers in the song they drink.
Our wisdom speaks from failing blood,
Our passion is too full in flood,
We want the key of his wild note
Of truthful in a tuneful throat,
The song seraphically free
Of taint of personality,
So pure that it salutes the suns,
The voice of one for millions,
In whom the millions rejoice
For giving their one spirit voice.

Yet men have we, whom we revere,
Now names, and men still housing here,
Whose lives, by many a battle-dint
Defaced, and grinding wheels on flint,
Yield substance, though they sing not, sweet
For song our highest heaven to greet :
Whom heavenly singing gives us new,
Enspheres them brilliant in our blue,
From firmest base to farthest leap,
Because their love of Earth is deep,
And they are warriors in accord
With life to serve, and pass reward,
So touching purest and so heard
In the brain's reflex of yon bird :
Wherefore their soul in me, or mine,
Through self-forgetfulness divine,
In them, that song aloft maintains,
To fill the sky and thrill the plains

With showerings drawn from human stores,
As he to silence nearer soars,
Extends the world at wings and dome,
More spacious making more our home,
Till lost on his aërial rings
In light, and then the fancy sings.

PHEOBUS WITH ADMETUS *

I

WHEN by Zeus relenting the mandate was revoked,
  Sentencing to exile the bright Sun-God,
Mindful were the ploughmen of who the steer had yoked,
  Who : and what a track showed the upturned sod !
Mindful were the shepherds as now the noon severe
  Bent a burning eyebrow to brown evetide,
How the rustic flute drew the silver to the sphere,
  Sister of his own, till her rays fell wide.[1]
        God ! of whom music
        And song and blood are pure,
        The day is never darkened
        That had thee here obscure.

II

Chirping none the scarlet cicalas crouched in ranks :
  Slack the thistle-head piled its down-silk grey :
Scarce the stony lizard sucked hollows in his flanks :
  Thick on spots of umbrage our drowsed flocks lay.
Sudden bowed the chestnuts beneath a wind unheard,
  Lengthened ran the grasses, the sky grew slate :
Then amid a swift flight of winged seed white as curd,
  Clear of limb a Youth smote the master's gate.
        God ! of whom music
        And song and blood are pure,
        The day is never darkened
        That had thee here obscure.

III

Water, first of singers, o'er rocky mount and mead,
   First of earthly singers, the sun-loved rill,
Sang of him, and flooded the ripples on the reed,
   Seeking whom to waken and what ear fill.
Water, sweetest soother to kiss a wound and cool,
   Sweetest and divinest, the sky-born brook,
Chuckled, with a whimper, and made a mirror-pool
   Round the guest we welcomed, the strange hand
     shook.
        God! of whom music
        And song and blood are pure,
        The day is never darkened
        That had thee here obscure.

IV

Many swarms of wild bees descended on our fields :
   Stately stood the wheatstalk with head bent high :
Big of heart we laboured at storing mighty yields,
   Wool and corn, and clusters to make men cry !
Hand-like rushed the vintage ; we strung the bellied
   skins
   Plump, and at the sealing the Youth's voice rose :
Maidens clung in circle, on little fists their chins ;
   Gentle beasties through pushed a cold long nose.
        God! of whom music
        And song and blood are pure,
        The day is never darkened
        That had thee here obscure.

V

Foot to fire in snowtime we trimmed the slender shaft :
   Often down the pit spied the lean wolf's teeth
Grin against his will, trapped by masterstrokes of craft ;
   Helpless in his froth-wrath as green logs seethe !
Safe the tender lambs tugged the teats, and winter sped
   Whirled before the crocus, the year's new gold.
Hung the hooky beak up aloft the arrowhead
   Reddened through his feathers for our dear fold.

God ! of whom music
And song and blood are pure,
The day is never darkened
That had thee here obscure.

VI

Tales we drank of giants at war with Gods above :
    Rocks were they to look on, and earth climbed air !
Tales of search for simples, and those who sought of love
    Ease because the creature was all too fair.
Pleasant ran our thinking that while our work was good,
    Sure as fruits for sweat would the praise come fast.
He that wrestled stoutest and tamed the billow-brood
    Danced in rings with girls, like a sail-flapped mast.
        God ! of whom music
        And song and blood are pure,
        The day is never darkened
        That had thee here obscure.

VII

Lo, the herb of healing, when once the herb is known,
    Shines in shady woods bright as new-sprung flame.
Ere the string was tightened we heard the mellow tone,
    After he had taught how the sweet sounds came.
Stretched about his feet, labour done, 'twas as you see
    Red pomegranates tumble and burst hard rind.
So began contention to give delight and be
    Excellent in things aimed to make life kind.
        God ! of whom music
        And song and blood are pure,
        The day is never darkened
        That had thee here obscure.

VIII

You with shelly horns, rams ! and promontory goats,
    You whose browsing beards dip in coldest dew !
Bulls, that walk the pastures in kingly-flashing coats !
    Laurel, ivy, vine, wreathed for feasts not few !
You that build the shade-roof, and you that court the
    rays,

You that leap besprinkling the rock stream-rent :
He has been our fellow, the morning of our days ;
    Us he chose for housemates, and this way went.
        God ! of whom music
        And song and blood are pure,
        The day is never darkened
        That had thee here obscure.

MELAMPUS *

I

WITH love exceeding a simple love of the things
    That glide in grasses and rubble of woody wreck ;
Or change their perch on a beat of quivering wings
    From branch to branch, only restful to pipe and peck ;
Or, bristled, curl at a touch their snouts in a ball ;
    Or cast their web between bramble and thorny hook ;
The good physician Melampus, loving them all,
    Among them walked, as a scholar who reads a book.

II

For him the woods were a home and gave him the key
    Of knowledge, thirst for their treasures in herbs and
        flowers.
The secrets held by the creatures nearer than we
    To earth he sought, and the link of their life with ours :
And where alike we are, unlike where, and the veined
    Division, veined parallel, of a blood that flows
In them, in us, from the source by man unattained
    Save marks he well what the mystical woods disclose.

III

And this he deemed might be boon of love to a breast
    Embracing tenderly each little motive shape,
The prone, the flitting, who seek their food whither best
    Their wits direct, whither best from their foes escape :
For closer drawn to our mother's natural milk,
    As babes they learn where her motherly help is great :
They know the juice for the honey, juice for the silk,
    And need they medical antidotes find them straight.

IV

Of earth and sun they are wise, they nourish their broods,
  Weave, build, hive, burrow and battle, take joy and pain
Like swimmers varying billows : never in woods
  Runs white insanity fleeing itself : all sane
The woods revolve : as the tree its shadowing limns
  To some resemblance in motion, the rooted life
Restrains disorder : you hear the primitive hymns
  Of earth in woods issue wild of the web of strife.

V

Now sleeping once on a day of marvellous fire,
  A brood of snakes he had cherished in grave regret
That death his people had dealt their dam and their sire,
  Through savage dread of them, crept to his neck, and set
Their tongues to lick him : the swift affectionate tongue
  Of each ran licking the slumberer : then his ears
A forked red tongue tickled shrewdly : sudden upsprung,
  He heard a voice piping : Ay, for he has no fears !

VI

A bird said that, in the notes of birds, and the speech
  Of men, it seemed : and another renewed : He moves
To learn and not to pursue, he gathers to teach ;
  He feeds his young as do we, and as we love loves.
No fears have I of a man who goes with his head
  To earth, chance looking aloft at us, kind of hand :
I feel to him as to earth of whom we are fed ;
  I pipe him much for his good could he understand.

VII

Melampus touched at his ears, laid finger on wrist :
  He was not dreaming, he sensibly felt and heard.
Above, through leaves, where the tree-twigs thick inter-
    twist,
  He spied the birds and the bill of the speaking bird.
His cushion mosses in shades of various green,
  The lumped, the antlered, he pressed, while the sunny
    snake
Slipped under : draughts he had drunk of clear Hippocrene,
  It seemed, and sat with a gift of the Gods awake.

VIII

Divinely thrilled was the man, exultingly full,
  As quick well-waters that come of the heart of earth,
Ere yet they dart in a brook, are one bubble-pool
  To light and sound, wedding both at the leap of birth.
The soul of light vivid shone, a stream within stream ;
  The soul of sound from a musical shell outflew ;
Where others hear but a hum and see but a beam,
  The tongue and eye of the fountain of life he knew.

IX

He knew the Hours : they were round him, laden with seed
  Of hours bestrewn upon vapour, and one by one
They winged as ripened in fruit the burden decreed
  For each to scatter ; they flushed like the buds in sun,
Bequeathing seed to successive similar rings,
  Their sisters, bearers to men of what men have earned :
He knew them, talked with the yet unreddened ; the stings,
  The sweets, they warmed at their bosoms divined, dis-
    cerned.

X

Not unsolicited, sought by diligent feet,
  By riddling fingers expanded, oft watched in growth
With brooding deep as the noon-ray's quickening wheat,
  Ere touch'd the pendulous flower of the plants of sloth,
The plants of rigidness, answered question and squeeze,
  Revealing wherefore it bloomed uninviting, bent,
Yet making harmony breathe of life and disease,
  The deeper chord of a wonderful instrument.

XI

So passed he luminous-eyed for earth and the fates
  We arm to bruise or caress us : his ears were charged
With tones of love in a whirl of voluble hates,
  With music wrought of distraction his heart enlarged.
Celestial-shining, though mortal, singer, though mute,
  He drew the Master of harmonies, voiced or stilled,
To seek him ; heard at the silent medicine-root
  A song, beheld in fulfilment the unfulfilled.

XII

Him Phoebus, lending to darkness colour and form
    Of light's excess, many lessons and counsels gave ;
Showed Wisdom lord of the human intricate swarm,
    And whence prophetic it looks on the hives that rave ;
And how acquired, of the zeal of love to acquire,
    And where it stands, in the centre of life a sphere ;
And Measure, mood of the lyre, the rapturous lyre,
    He said was Wisdom, and struck him the notes to hear.

XIII

Sweet, sweet : 'twas glory of vision, honey, the breeze
    In heat, the run of the river on root and stone,
All senses joined, as the sister Pierides
    Are one, uplifting their chorus, the Nine, his own.[1]
In stately order, evolved of sound into sight,
    From sight to sound intershifting, the man descried
The growths of earth, his adored, like day out of night,
    Ascend in song, seeing nature and song allied.

XIV

And there vitality, there, there solely in song,
    Resides, where earth and her uses to men, their needs,
Their forceful cravings, the theme are : there is it strong,
    The Master said : and the studious eye that reads
(Yea, even as earth to the crown of Gods on the mount)
    In links divine with the lyrical tongue is bound.
Pursue thy craft : it is music drawn of a fount
    To spring perennial ; well-spring is common ground.

XV

Melampus dwelt among men : physician and sage,
    He served them, loving them, healing them ; sick or
        maimed
Or them that frenzied in some delirious rage
    Outran the measure, his juice of the woods reclaimed.
He played on men, as his master, Phoebus, on strings
    Melodious : as the God did he drive and check,
Through love exceeding a simple love of the things
    That glide in grasses and rubble of woody wreck.

LOVE IN THE VALLEY

[The first version of ' Love in the Valley,' which appeared among the ' Pastorals ' in the *Poems* of 1851, can be found on p. 173 below.]

UNDER yonder beech-tree single on the green-sward,
  Couched with her arms behind her golden head,
Knees and tresses folded to slip and ripple idly,
  Lies my young love sleeping in the shade.
Had I the heart to slide an arm beneath her,
  Press her parting lips as her waist I gather slow,
Waking in amazement she could not but embrace me :
  Then would she hold me and never let me go ?

                *   *   *

Shy as the squirrel and wayward as the swallow,
  Swift as the swallow along the river's light
Circleting the surface to meet his mirrored winglets,
  Fleeter she seems in her stay than in her flight.
Shy as the squirrel that leaps among the pine-tops,
  Wayward as the swallow overhead at set of sun,
She whom I love is hard to catch and conquer,
  Hard, but O the glory of the winning were she won !

                *   *   *

When her mother tends her before the laughing mirror,
  Tying up her laces, looping up her hair,
Often she thinks, were this wild thing wedded,
  More love should I have, and much less care.
When her mother tends her before the lighted mirror,
  Loosening her laces, combing down her curls,
Often she thinks, were this wild thing wedded,
  I should miss but one for many boys and girls.

                *   *   *

Heartless she is as the shadow in the meadows
  Flying to the hills on a blue and breezy noon.
No, she is athirst and drinking up her wonder :
  Earth to her is young as the slip of the new moon.

Deals she an unkindness, 'tis but her rapid measure,
   Even as in a dance ; and her smile can heal no less :
Like the swinging May-cloud that pelts the flowers with
      hailstones
Off a sunny border, she was made to bruise and bless.

            *   *   *

Lovely are the curves of the white owl sweeping
   Wavy in the dusk lit by one large star.
Lone on the fir-branch, his rattle-note unvaried,
   Brooding o'er the gloom, spins the brown eve-jar.
Darker grows the valley, more and more forgetting :
   So were it with me if forgetting could be willed.
Tell the grassy hollow that holds the bubbling well-spring
   Tell it to forget the source that keeps it filled.

            *   *   *

Stepping down the hill with her fair companions,
   Arm in arm, all against the raying West,
Boldly she sings, to the merry tune she marches,
   Brave in her shape, and sweeter unpossessed.
Sweeter, for she is what my heart first awaking
   Whispered the world was ; morning light is she.
Love that so desires would fain keep her changeless ;
   Fain would fling the net, and fain have her free.

            *   *   *

Happy happy time, when the white star hovers
   Low over dim fields fresh with bloomy dew,
Near the face of dawn, that draws athwart the darkness,
   Threading it with colour, like yewberries the yew.
Thicker crowd the shades as the grave East deepens
   Glowing, and with crimson a long cloud swells.
Maiden still the morn is ; and strange she is, and secret ;
   Strange her eyes ; her cheeks are cold as cold sea-shells.

            *   *   *

Sunrays, leaning on our southern hills and lighting
   Wild cloud-mountains that drag the hills along,
Oft ends the day of your shifting brilliant laughter
   Chill as a dull face frowning on a song.

Ay, but shows the South-West a ripple-feathered bosom
   Blown to silver while the clouds are shaken and ascend
Scaling the mid-heavens as they stream, there comes a sunset
   Rich, deep like love in beauty without end.

        *   *   *

When at dawn she sighs, and like an infant to the window
   Turns grave eyes craving light, released from dreams,
Beautiful she looks, like a white water-lily
   Bursting out of bud in havens of the streams.
When from bed she rises clothed from neck to ankle
   In her long nightgown sweet as boughs of May,
Beautiful she looks, like a tall garden lily
   Pure from the night, and splendid for the day.

        *   *   *

Mother of the dews, dark eye-lashed twilight,
   Low-lidded twilight, o'er the valley's brim,
Rounding on thy breast sings the dew-delighted skylark,
   Clear as though the dewdrops had their voice in him.
Hidden where the rose-flush drinks the rayless planet,
   Fountain-full he pours the spraying fountain-showers.
Let me hear her laughter, I would have her ever
   Cool as dew in twilight, the lark above the flowers.

        *   *   *

All the girls are out with their baskets for the primrose ;
   Up lanes, woods through, they troop in joyful bands.
My sweet leads : she knows not why, but now she loiters,
   Eyes the bent anemones, and hangs her hands.
Such a look will tell that the violets are peeping,
   Coming the rose : and unaware a cry
Springs in her bosom for odours and for colour,
   Covert and the nightingale ; she knows not why.

        *   *   *

Kerchiefed head and chin she darts between her tulips,
   Streaming like a willow grey in arrowy rain :
Some bend beaten cheek to gravel, and their angel
   She will be ; she lifts them, and on she speeds again.
Black the driving raincloud breasts the iron gateway :
   She is forth to cheer a neighbour lacking mirth.
So when sky and grass met rolling dumb for thunder
   Saw I once a white dove, sole light of earth.

G

Prim little scholars are the flowers of her garden,
  Trained to stand in rows, and asking if they please.
I might love them well but for loving more the wild ones :
  O my wild ones ! they tell me more than these.
You, my wild one, you tell of honied field-rose,
  Violet, blushing eglantine in life ; and even as they,
They by the wayside are earnest of your goodness,
  You are of life's on the banks that line the way.

*   *   *

Peering at her chamber the white crowns the red rose,
  Jasmine winds the porch with stars two and three.
Parted is the window ; she sleeps ; the starry jasmine
  Breathes a falling breath that carries thoughts of me.
Sweeter unpossessed, have I said of her my sweetest ?
  Not while she sleeps : while she sleeps the jasmine
    breathes,
Luring her to love ; she sleeps ; the starry jasmine
  Bears me to her pillow under white rose-wreaths.

*   *   *

Yellow with birdfoot-trefoil are the grass-glades ;
  Yellow with cinquefoil of the dew-grey leaf ;
Yellow with stonecrop ; the moss-mounds are yellow ;
  Blue-necked the wheat sways, yellowing to the sheaf.
Green-yellow bursts from the copse the laughing yaffle ;
  Sharp as a sickle is the edge of shade and shine :
Earth in her heart laughs looking at the heavens,
  Thinking of the harvest : I look and think of mine.

*   *   *

This I may know : her dressing and undressing
  Such a change of light shows as when the skies in sport
Shift from cloud to moonlight ; or edging over thunder
  Slips a ray of sun ; or sweeping into port
White sails furl ; or on the ocean borders
  White sails lean along the waves leaping green.
Visions of her shower before me, but from eyesight
  Guarded she would be like the sun were she seen.

*   *   *

Front door and back of the mossed old farmhouse
  Open with the morn, and in a breezy link
Freshly sparkles garden to stripe-shadowed orchard,
  Green across a rill where on sand the minnows wink.

Busy in the grass the early sun of summer
   Swarms, and the blackbird's mellow fluting notes
Call my darling up with round and roguish challenge :
   Quaintest, richest carol of all the singing throats !

     *   *   *

Cool was the woodside ; cool as her white dairy
   Keeping sweet the cream-pan ; and there the boys from
      school,
Cricketing below, rushed brown and red with sunshine ;
   O the dark translucence of the deep-eyed cool !
Spying from the farm, herself she fetched a pitcher
   Full of milk, and tilted for each in turn the beak.
Then a little fellow, mouth up and on tiptoe,
   Said, ' I will kiss you ' : she laughed and leaned her cheek.

     *   *   *

Doves of the fir-wood walling high our red roof
   Through the long noon coo, crooning through the coo.
Loose droop the leaves, and down the sleepy roadway
   Sometimes pipes a chaffinch ; loose droops the blue.
Cows flap a slow tail knee-deep in the river,
   Breathless, given up to sun and gnat and fly.
Nowhere is she seen ; and if I see her nowhere,
   Lightning may come, straight rains and tiger sky.

     *   *   *

O the golden sheaf, the rustling treasure-armful !
   O the nutbrown tresses nodding interlaced !
O the treasure-tresses one another over
   Nodding ! O the girdle slack about the waist !
Slain are the poppies that shot their random scarlet
   Quick amid the wheatears : wound about the waist,
Gathered, see these brides of Earth one blush of ripeness !
   O the nutbrown tresses nodding interlaced !

     *   *   *

Large and smoky red the sun's cold disk drops,
   Clipped by naked hills, on violet shaded snow :
Eastward large and still lights up a bower of moonrise,
   Whence at her leisure steps the moon aglow.
Nightlong on black print-branches our beech-tree
   Gazes in this whiteness : nightlong could I.
Here may life on death or death on life be painted.
   Let me clasp her soul to know she cannot die !

Gossips count her faults ; they scour a narrow chamber
  Where there is no window, read not heaven or her.
' When she was a tiny,' one aged woman quavers,
  Plucks at my heart and leads me by the ear.
Faults she had once as she learnt to run and tumbled :
  Faults of feature some see, beauty not complete.
Yet, good gossips, beauty that makes holy
  Earth and air, may have faults from head to feet.

     *   *   *

Hither she comes ; she comes to me ; she lingers,
  Deepens her brown eyebrows, while in new surprise
High rise the lashes in wonder of a stranger ;
  Yet am I the light and living of her eyes.
Something friends have told her fills her heart to brimming,
  Nets her in her blushes, and wounds her, and tames.—
Sure of her haven, O like a dove alighting,
  Arms up, she dropped : our souls were in our names.

     *   *   *

Soon will she lie like a white-frost sunrise.
  Yellow oats and brown wheat, barley pale as rye,
Long since your sheaves have yielded to the thresher,
  Felt the girdle loosened, seen the tresses fly.
Soon will she lie like a blood-red sunset.
  Swift with the to-morrow, green-winged Spring !
Sing from the South-West, bring her back the truants,
  Nightingale and swallow, song and dipping wing.

     *   *   *

Soft new beech-leaves, up to beamy April
  Spreading bough on bough a primrose mountain, you,
Lucid in the moon, raise lilies to the skyfields,
  Youngest green transfused in silver shining through :
Fairer than the lily, than the wild white cherry :
  Fair as in image my seraph love appears
Borne to me by dreams when dawn is at my eyelids :
  Fair as in the flesh she swims to me on tears.

     *   *   *

Could I find a place to be alone with heaven,
  I would speak my heart out : heaven is my need.
Every woodland tree is flushing like the dogwood,
  Flashing like the whitebeam, swaying like the reed.

Flushing like the dogwood crimson in October ;
　Streaming like the flag-reed South-West blown ;
Flashing as in gusts the sudden-lighted whitebeam :
　All seem to know what is for heaven alone.

THE THREE SINGERS TO YOUNG BLOOD *

CAROLS nature, counsel men.
Different notes as rook from wren
Hear we when our steps begin,
And the choice is cast within,
Where a robber raven's tale
Urges passion's nightingale.

Hark to the three. Chimed they in one,
Life were music of the sun.
Liquid first, and then the caw,
Then the cry that knows not law.

I

As the birds do, so do we,
Bill our mate, and choose our tree.
Swift to building work addressed,
Any straw will help a nest.
Mates are warm, and this is truth,
Glad the young that come of youth.
They have bloom i' the blood and sap
Chilling at no thunder-clap.
Man and woman on the thorn
Trust not Earth, and have her scorn.
They who in her lead confide,
Wither me if they spread not wide !
Look for aid to little things,
You will get them quick as wings,
Thick as feathers ; would you feed,
Take the leap that springs the need.

II

Contemplate the rutted road :
Life is both a lure and goad.
Each to hold in measure just,
Trample appetite to dust.
Mark the fool and wanton spin :
Keep to harness as a skin.
Ere you follow nature's lead,
Of her powers in you have heed ;
Else a shiverer you will find
You have challenged humankind.
Mates are chosen marketwise :
Coolest bargainer best buys.
Leap not, nor let leap the heart :
Trot your track, and drag your cart.
So your end may be in wool,
Honoured, and with manger full.

III

O the rosy light ! it fleets,
Dearer dying than all sweets.
That is life : it waves and goes ;
Solely in that cherished Rose
Palpitates, or else 'tis death.
Call it love with all thy breath.
Love ! it lingers : Love ! it nears :
Love ! O Love ! the Rose appears,
Blushful, magic, reddening air.
Now the choice is on thee : dare !
Mortal seems the touch, but makes
Immortal the hand that takes.
Feel what sea within thee shames
Of its force all other claims,
Drowns them. Clasp ! the world will be
Heavenly Rose to swelling sea.

THE ORCHARD AND THE HEATH *

I CHANCED upon an early walk to spy
A troop of children through an orchard gate :
　　The boughs hung low, the grass was high ;
　　They had but to lift hands or wait
For fruits to fill them ; fruits were all their sky.

They shouted, running on from tree to tree,
And played the game the wind plays, on and round.
　　'Twas visible invisible glee
　　Pursuing ; and a fountain's sound
Of laughter spouted, pattering fresh on me.

I could have watched them till the daylight fled,
Their pretty bower made such a light of day.
　　A small one tumbling sang, ' Oh ! head ! '
　　The rest to comfort her straightway
Seized on a branch and thumped down apples red.

The tiny creature flashing through green grass,
And laughing with her feet and eyes among
　　Fresh apples, while a little lass
　　Over as o'er breeze-ripples hung :
That sight I saw, and passed as aliens pass.

My footpath left the pleasant farms and lanes,
Soft cottage-smoke, straight cocks a-crow, gay flowers ;
　　Beyond the wheel-ruts of the wains,
　　Across a heath I walked for hours,
And met its rival tenants, rays and rains.

Still in my view mile-distant firs appeared,
When, under a patched channel-bank enriched
　　With foxglove whose late bells dropped seared,
　　Behold, a family had pitched
Their camp, and labouring the low tent upreared.

Here, too, were many children, quick to scan
A new thing coming ; swarthy cheeks, white teeth ;
  In many-coloured rags they ran,
  Like iron runlets of the heath.
Dispersed lay broth-pot, sticks, and drinking-can.

Three girls, with shoulders like a boat at sea
Tipped sideways by the wave (their clothing slid
  From either ridge unequally).
  Lean, swift and voluble, bestrid
A starting-point, unfrocked to the bent knee.

They raced ; their brothers yelled them on, and broke
In act to follow, but as one they snuffed
  Wood-fumes, and by the fire that spoke
  Of provender its pale flame puffed,
And rolled athwart dwarf furzes grey-blue smoke.

Soon on the dark edge of a ruddier gleam,
The mother-pot perusing, all, stretched flat,
  Paused for its bubbling-up supreme :
  A dog upright in circle sat,
And oft his nose went with the flying steam.

I turned and looked on heaven awhile, where now
The moor-faced sunset broaden'd with red light ;
  Threw high aloft a golden bough,
  And seemed the desert of the night
Far down with mellow orchards to endow.

EARTH AND MAN *

I

On her great venture, Man,
Earth gazes while her fingers dint the breast
Which is his well of strength, his home of rest,
And fair to scan.[1]

II

More aid than that embrace,
That nourishment, she cannot give : his heart
Involves his fate ; and she who urged the start
Abides the race.

III

For he is in the lists
Contentious with the elements, whose dower
First sprang him ; for swift vultures to devour
If he desists.

IV

His breath of instant thirst
Is warning of a creature matched with strife,
To meet it as a bride, or let fall life
On life's accursed.

V

No longer forth he bounds
The lusty animal, afield to roam,
But peering in Earth's entrails, where the gnome
Strange themes propounds.

VI

By hunger sharply sped
To grasp at weapons ere he learns their use,
In each new ring he bears a giant's thews,
An infant's head.

VII

And ever that old task
Of reading what he is and whence he came,
Whither to go, finds wilder letters flame
Across her mask.

VIII

She hears his wailful prayer,
When now to the Invisible [2] he raves
To rend him from her, now of his mother craves
Her calm, her care.

IX

The thing that shudders most
Within him is the burden of his cry.
Seen of his dread, she is to his blank eye
The eyeless Ghost.

X

Or sometimes she will seem
Heavenly, but her blush, soon wearing white,
Veils like a gorsebush in a web of blight,
With gold-buds dim.

XI

Once worshipped Prime of Powers,
She still was the Implacable : as a beast,
She struck him down and dragged him from the feast
She crowned with flowers.

XII

Her pomp of glorious hues,
Her revelries of ripeness, her kind smile,
Her songs, her peeping faces, lure awhile
With symbol-clues.

XIII

The mystery she holds
For him, inveterately he strains to see,
And sight of his obtuseness is the key
Among those folds.

XIV

He may entreat, aspire,
He may despair, and she has never heed.
She drinking his warm sweat will soothe his need,
Not his desire.

XV

She prompts him to rejoice,
Yet scares him on the threshold with the shroud.
He deems her cherishing of her best-endowed [3]
A wanton's choice.

XVI

Albeit thereof he has found
Firm roadway between lustfulness and pain ;
Has half transferred the battle to his brain,
From bloody ground ;

XVII

He will not read her good,
Or wise, but with the passion Self obscures ;
Through that old devil of the thousand lures,
Through that dense hood :

XVIII

Through terror, through distrust ;
The greed to touch, to view, to have, to live :
Through all that makes of him a sensitive
Abhorring dust.

XIX

Behold his wormy home !
And he the wind-whipped, anywhither wave
Crazily tumbled on a shingle-grave
To waste in foam.

XX

Therefore the wretch inclines
Afresh to the Invisible, who, he saith,
Can raise him high : with vows of living faith
For little signs.

XXI

Some signs he must demand,
Some proofs of slaughtered nature ; some prized few,
To satisfy the senses it is true,
And in his hand,

XXII

This miracle which saves
Himself, himself doth from extinction clutch,
By virtue of his worth, contrasting much
With brutes and knaves.

XXIII

From dust, of him abhorred,
He would be snatched by Grace discovering worth.
' Sever me from the hollowness of Earth !
Me take, dear Lord ! '

XXIV

She hears him. Him she owes
For half her loveliness a love well won
By work that lights the shapeless and the dun,
Their common foes.

XXV

He builds the soaring spires,
That sing his soul in stone : of her he draws,
Though blind to her, by spelling at her laws,
Her purest fires.

XXVI

Through him has she exchanged,
For the gold harvest-robes, the mural crown,
Her haggard quarry-features and thick frown
Where monsters ranged.

XXVII

And order, high discourse,
And decency, than which is life less dear,
She has of him : the lyre of language clear,
Love's tongue and source.

XXVIII

She hears him, and can hear
With glory in his gains by work achieved :
With grief for grief that is the unperceived
In her so near.

XXIX

If he aloft for aid
Imploring storms, her essence is the spur.
His cry to heaven is a cry to her
He would evade.

XXX

Not elsewhere can he tend.
Those are her rules which bid him wash foul sins ;
Those her revulsions from the skull that grins
To ape his end.

XXXI

And her desires are those
For happiness, for lastingness, for light.
'Tis she who kindles in his haunting night
The hoped dawn-rose.

XXXII

Fair fountains of the dark
Daily she waves him, that his inner dream
May clasp amid the glooms a springing beam,
A quivering lark :

XXXIII

This life and her to know
For Spirit : with awakenedness of glee
To feel stern joy her origin : not he
The child of woe.

XXXIV

But that the senses still
Usurp the station of their issue mind,
He would have burst the chrysalis of the blind :
As yet he will ;

XXXV

As yet he will, she prays,
Yet will when his distempered devil of Self ;—
The glutton for her fruits, the wily elf
In shifting rays ;

XXXVI

That captain of the scorned ;
The coveter of life in soul and shell,
The fratricide, the thief, the infidel,
The hoofed and horned ;—

XXXVII

He singularly doomed
To what he execrates and writhes to shun ;—
When fire has passed him vapour to the sun,
And sun relumed,

XXXVIII

Then shall the horrid pall
Be lifted, and a spirit nigh divine,
' Live in thy offspring as I live in mine,'
Will hear her call.

XXXIX

Whence looks he on a land
Whereon his labour is a carven page ;
And forth from heritage to heritage
Nought writ on sand.

XL

His fables of the Above,
And his gapped readings of the crown and sword,
The hell detested and the heaven adored,
The hate, the love.

XLI

The bright wing, the black hoof,
He shall peruse, from Reason not disjoined,
And never unfaith clamouring to be coined
To faith by proof.

XLII

She her just Lord may view,
Not he, her creature, till his soul has yearned
With all her gifts to reach the light discerned
Her spirit through.[4]

XLIII

Then in him time shall run
As in the hour that to young sunlight crows ;
And—' If thou hast good faith it can repose,'
She tells her son.

Meanwhile on him, her chief
Expression, her great word of life, looks she ;
Twi-minded of him, as the waxing tree,
Or dated leaf.

THE SONG OF THEODOLINDA *

I

QUEEN THEODOLIND has built
In the earth a furnace-bed :
There the Traitor Nail that spilt
Blood of the anointed Head,
Red of heat, resolves in shame :
White of heat, awakes to flame.
  Beat, beat ! white of heat,
  Red of heat, beat, beat !

II

Mark the skeleton of fire
Lightening from its thunder-roof :
So comes this that saw expire
Him we love, for our behoof !
Red of heat, O white of heat,
This from off the Cross we greet.

III

Brown-cowled hammermen around
Nerve their naked arms to strike
Death with Resurrection crowned,
Each upon that cruel spike.
Red of heat the furnace leaps,
White of heat transfigured sleeps.

IV

Hard against the furnace core
Holds the Queen her streaming eyes :
Lo ! that thing of piteous gore
In the lap of radiance lies,
Red of heat, as when He takes,
White of heat, whom earth forsakes.

V

Forth with it, and crushing ring
Iron hymns, for men to hear
Echoes of the deeds that sting
Earth into its graves, and fear !
Red of heat, He maketh thus,
White of heat, a crown of us.

VI

This, that killed Thee, kissed Thee, Lord !
Touched Thee, and we touch it : dear,
Dark it is ; adored, abhorred :
Vilest, yet most sainted here.
Red of heat, O white of heat,
In it hell and heaven meet.

VII

I behold our morning day
When they chased Him out with rods
Up to where this traitor lay
Thirsting ; and the blood was God's !
Red of heat, it shall be pressed,
White of heat, once on my breast !

VIII

Quick ! the reptile in me shrieks,
Not the soul. Again ; the Cross
Burn there. Oh ! this pain it wreaks
Rapture is : pain is not loss.
Red of heat, the tooth of Death,
White of heat, has caught my breath.

IX

Brand me, bite me, bitter thing !
Thus He felt, and thus I am
One with Him in suffering,
One with Him in bliss, the Lamb.
Red of heat, O white of heat,
Thus is bitterness made sweet.

X

Now am I, who bear that stamp
Scorched in me, the living sign
Sole on earth—the lighted lamp
Of the dreadful day divine.
White of heat, beat on it fast !
Red of heat, its shape has passed.

XI

Out in angry sparks they fly,
They that sentenced Him to bleed :
Pontius and his troop : they die,
Damned for ever for the deed !
White of heat in vain they soar :
Red of heat they strew the floor.

XII

Fury on it ! have its debt !
Thunder on the Hill accurst,
Golgotha, be ye ! and sweat
Blood, and thirst the Passion's thirst.
Red of heat and white of heat,
Champ it like fierce teeth that eat.

XIII

Strike it as the ages crush
Towers ! for while a shape is seen
I am rivalled. Quench its blush,
Devil ! But it crowns me Queen,
Red of heat, as none before,
White of heat, the circlet wore.

XIV

Lowly I will be, and quail,
Crawling, with a beggar's hand :
On my breast the branded Nail,
On my head the iron band.
Red of heat, are none so base !
White of heat, none know such grace !

H

XV

In their heaven the sainted hosts,
Robed in violet unflecked,
Gaze on humankind as ghosts :
I draw down a ray direct.
Red of heat, across my brow,
White of heat, I touch Him now.

XVI

Robed in violet, robed in gold,
Robed in pearl, they make our dawn.
What am I to them ? Behold
What ye are to me, and fawn.
Red of heat, be humble, ye !
White of heat, O teach it me !

XVII

Martyrs ! hungry peaks in air,
Rent with lightnings, clad with snow,
Crowned with stars ! you strip me bare,
Pierce me, shame me, stretch me low,
Red of heat, but it may be,
White of heat, some envy me !

XVIII

O poor enviers ! God's own gifts
Have a devil for the weak.
Yea, the very force that lifts
Finds the vessel's secret leak.
Red of heat, I rise o'er all :
White of heat, I faint, I fall.

XIX

Those old Martyrs sloughed their pride,
Taking humbleness like mirth.
I am to His Glory tied,
I that witness Him on earth !
Red of heat, my pride of dust,
White of heat, feeds fire in trust.

XX

Kindle me to constant fire,
Lest the nail be but a nail !
Give me wings of great desire,
Lest I look within, and fail !
Red of heat, the furnace light
White of heat, fix on my sight.

XXI

Never for the Chosen peace !
Know, by me tormented know,
Never shall the wrestling cease
Till with our outlasting Foe,
Red of heat, to white of heat
Roll we to the Godhead's feet !
    Beat, beat ! white of heat,
    Red of heat, beat, beat !

THE YOUNG PRINCESS *

A BALLAD OF OLD LAWS OF LOVE

I *

I

WHEN the South sang like a nightingale
    Above a bower in May,
The training of Love's vine of flame
Was writ in laws, for lord and dame
    To say their yea and nay.

II

When the South sang like a nightingale
    Across the flowering night,
And lord and dame held gentle sport,
There came a young princess to Court,
    A frost of beauty white.

III

The South sang like a nightingale
    To thaw her glittering dream :
No vine of Love her bosom gave,
She drank no wine of Love, but grave
    She held them to Love's theme.

IV

The South grew all a nightingale
    Beneath a moon unmoved :
Like the banner of war she led them on ;
She left them to lie, like the light that has gone
    From wine-cups overproved.

V

When the South was a fervid nightingale,
    And she a chilling moon,
'Twas pity to see on the garden swards,
Against Love's laws, those rival lords
    As willow-wands lie strewn.

VI

The South had throat of a nightingale
    For her, the young princess :
She gave no vine of Love to rear,
Love's wine drank not, yet bent her ear
    To themes of Love no less.

II *

I

The lords of the Court they sighed heart-sick,
    Heart-free Lord Dusiote laughed :
I prize her no more than a fling o' the dice,
But, or shame to my manhood, a lady of ice,
    We master her by craft !

II

Heart-sick the lords of joyance yawned,
    Lord Dusiote laughed heart-free :
I count her as much as a crack o' my thumb,
But, or shame of my manhood, to me she shall come
    Like the bird to roost in the tree !

III

At dead of night when the palace-guard
    Had passed the measured rounds,
The young princess awoke to feel
A shudder of blood at the crackle of steel
    Within the garden-bounds.

IV

It ceased, and she thought of whom was need,
    The friar or the leech ;
When lo, stood her tirewoman breathless by :
Lord Dusiote, madam, to death is nigh,
    Of you he would have speech.

V

He prays you, of your gentleness,
    To light him to his dark end.
The princess rose, and forth she went,
For charity was her intent,
    Devoutly to befriend.

VI

Lord Dusiote hung on his good squire's arm,
    The priest beside him knelt :
A weeping handkerchief was pressed
To stay the red flood at his breast,
    And bid cold ladies melt.

VII

O lady, though you are ice to men,
    All pure to heaven as light
Within the dew within the flower,
Of you 'tis whispered that love has power
    When secret is the night.

VIII

I have silenced the slanderers, peace to their souls !
  Save one was too cunning for me.
I die, whose love is late avowed,
He lives, who boasts the lily has bowed
  To the oath of a bended knee.

IX

Lord Dusiote drew breath with pain,
  And she with pain drew breath :
On him she looked, on his like above ;
She flew in the folds of a marvel of love,
  Revealed to pass to death.

X

You are dying, O great-hearted lord,
  You are dying for me, she cried ;
O take my hand, O take my kiss,
And take of your right, for love like this,
  The vow that plights me bride.

XI

She bade the priest recite his words
  While hand in hand were they,
Lord Dusiote's soul to waft to bliss ;
He had her hand, her vow, her kiss,
  And his body was borne away.

III *

I

Lord Dusiote sprang from priest and squire ;
  He gazed at her lighted room :
The laughter in his heart grew slack ;
He knew not the force that pushed him back
  From her and the morn in bloom.

II

Like a drowned man's length on the strong flood-
    tide,
  Like the shade of a bird in the sun,
He fled from his lady whom he might claim
As ghost, and who made the daybeams flame
    To scare what he had done.

III

There was grief at Court for one so gay,
  Though he was a lord less keen
For training the vine than at vintage-press ;
But in her soul the young princess
    Believed that love had been.

IV

Lord Dusiote fled the Court and land,
  He crossed the woeful seas,
Till his traitorous doing seemed clearer to burn,
And the lady beloved drew his heart for return,
    Like the banner of war in the breeze.

V

He neared the palace, he spied the Court,
  And music he heard, and they told
Of foreign lords arrived to bring
The nuptial gifts of a bridegroom king
    To the princess grave and cold.

VI

The masque and the dance were cloud on wave,
  And down the masque and the dance
Lord Dusiote stepped from dame to dame,
And to the young princess he came,
    With a bow and a burning glance.

VII

Do you take a new husband to-morrow, lady ?
  She shrank as at prick of steel.
Must the first yield place to the second, he sighed.
Her eyes were like the grave that is wide
    For the corpse from head to heel.

VIII

My lady, my love, that little hand
    Has mine ringed fast in plight :
I bear for your lips a lawful thirst,
And as justly the second should follow the first,
    I come to your door this night.

IX

If a ghost should come a ghost will go :
    No more the lady said,
Save that ever when he in wrath began
To swear by the faith of a living man,
    She answered him, You are dead.

IV *

I

The soft night-wind went laden to death
    With smell of the orange in flower ;
The light leaves prattled to neighbour ears ;
The bird of the passion sang over his tears ;
    The night named hour by hour.

II

Sang loud, sang low the rapturous bird
    Till the yellow hour was nigh,
Behind the folds of a darker cloud :
He chuckled, he sobbed, alow, aloud ;
    The voice between earth and sky.

III

O will you, will you, women are weak ;
    The proudest are yielding mates
For a forward foot and a tongue of fire :
So thought Lord Dusiote's trusty squire,
    At watch by the palace-gates.

IV

The song of the bird was wine in his blood,
 And woman the odorous bloom :
His master's great adventure stirred
Within him to mingle the bloom and bird,
 And morn ere its coming illume.

V

Beside him strangely a piece of the dark
 Had moved, and the undertones
Of a priest in prayer, like a cavernous wave,
He heard, as were there a soul to save
 For urgency now in the groans.

VI

No priest was hired for the play this night :
 And the squire tossed head like a deer
At sniff of the tainted wind ; he gazed
Where cresset-lamps in a door were raised,
 Belike on a passing bier.

VII

All cloaked and masked, with naked blades,
 That flashed of a judgement done,
The lords of the Court, from the palace-door,
Came issuing silently, bearers four,
 And flat on their shoulders one.

VIII

They marched the body to squire and priest,
 They lowered it sad to earth :
The priest they gave the burial dole
Bade wrestle hourly for his soul,
 Who was a lord of worth.

IX

One said, farewell to a gallant knight !
 And one, but a restless ghost !
'Tis a year and a day since in this place
He died, sped high by a lady of grace,
 To join the blissful host.

X

Not vainly on us she charged her cause,
The lady whom we revere
For faith in the mask of a love untrue
To the Love we honour, the Love her due,
The Love we have vowed to rear.

XI

A trap for the sweet tooth, lures for the light,
For the fortress defiant a mine :
Right well ! But not in the South, princess,
Shall the lady snared of her nobleness
Ever shamed or a captive pine.

XII

When the South had voice of a nightingale
Above a Maying bower,
On the heights of Love walked radiant peers ;
The bird of the passion sang over his tears
To the breeze and the orange-flower.

YOUNG REYNARD

I

GRACEFULLEST leaper, the dappled fox-cub
Curves over brambles with berries and buds,
Light as a bubble that flies from the tub,
Whisked by the laundry-wife out of her suds.
Wavy he comes, woolly, all at his ease,
Elegant, fashioned to foot with the deuce ;
Nature's own prince of the dance : then he sees
Me, and retires as if making excuse.

II

Never closed minuet courtlier ! Soon
Cub-hunting troops were abroad, and a yelp
Told of sure scent : ere the stroke upon noon
Reynard the younger lay far beyond help.

Wild, my poor friend, has the fate to be chased ;
Civil will conquer : were 't other 'twere worse ;
Fair, by the flushed early morning embraced,
Haply you live a day longer in verse.

MANFRED *

I

PROJECTED from the bilious Childe,
This clatterjaw his foot could set
On Alps, without a breast beguiled
To glow in shedding rascal sweat.
Somewhere about his grinder teeth,
He mouthed of thoughts that grilled beneath,
And summoned Nature to her feud
With bile and buskin Attitude.

II

Considerably was the world
Of spinsterdom and clergy racked
While he his hinted horrors hurled,
And she pictorially attacked.
A duel hugeous. Tragic ? Ho !
The cities, not the mountains, blow
Such bladders ; in their shapes confessed
An after-dinner's indigest.

HERNANI *

CISTERCIANS might crack their sides
With laughter, and exemption get,
At sight of heroes clasping brides,
And hearing—O the horn ! the horn !
The horn of their obstructive debt !

But quit the stage, that note applies
For sermons cosmopolitan,
Hernani. Have we filched our prize,
Forgetting . . . ? O the horn ! the horn !
The horn of the Old Gentleman !

THE NUPTIALS OF ATTILA *

I

FLAT as to an eagle's eye,
    Earth hung under Attila.
Sign for carnage gave he none.
In the peace of his disdain,
Sun and rain, and rain and sun,
Cherished men to wax again,
Crawl, and in their manner die.
On his people stood a frost.
Like the charger cut in stone,
Rearing stiff, the warrior host,
Which had life from him alone,
Craved the trumpet's eager note,
As the bridled earth the Spring.
Rusty was the trumpet's throat.
He let chief and prophet rave ;
Venturous earth around him string
Threads of grass and slender rye,
Wave them, and untrampled wave.
O for the time when God did cry,
    Eye and have, my Attila !

II

Scorn of conquest filled like sleep
Him that drank of havoc deep
When the Green Cat pawed the globe :
When the horsemen from his bow
Shot in sheaves and made the foe
Crimson fringes of a robe,
Trailed o'er towns and fields in woe ;
When they streaked the rivers red,
When the saddle was the bed.
    Attila, my Attila !

III

He breathed peace and pulled a flower.
    Eye and have, my Attila !
This was the damsel Ildico,
Rich in bloom until that hour :

Shyer than the forest doe
Twinkling slim through branches green.
Yet the shyest shall be seen.
    Make the bed for Attila !

IV

Seen of Attila, desired,
She was led to him straightway :
Radiantly was she attired ;
Rifled lands were her array,
Jewels bled from weeping crowns,
Gold of woeful fields and towns.
She stood pallid in the light.
How she walked, how withered white,
From the blessing to the board,
She who should have proudly blushed,
Women whispered, asking why,
Hinting of a youth, and hushed.
Was it terror of her lord ?
Was she childish ? was she sly ?
Was it the bright mantle's dye
Drained her blood to hues of grief
Like the ash that shoots the spark ?
See the green tree all in leaf :
See the green tree stripped of bark !—
    Make the bed for Attila !

V

Round the banquet-table's load
Scores of iron horsemen rode ;
Chosen warriors, keen and hard ;
Grain of threshing battle-dints ;
Attila's fierce body-guard,
Smelling war like fire in flints.
Grant them peace be fugitive !
Iron-capped and iron-heeled,
Each against his fellow's shield
Smote the spear-head, shouting, Live,
    Attila ! my Attila !

Eagle, eagle of our breed,
Eagle, beak the lamb, and feed !
Have her, and unleash us ! live,
    Attila ! my Attila !

VI

He was of the blood to shine
Bronze in joy, like skies that scorch
Beaming with the goblet wine
In the wavering of the torch,
Looked he backward on his bride.
    Eye and have, my Attila !
Fair in her wide robe was she :
Where the robe and vest divide,
Fair she seemed surpassingly :
Soft, yet vivid as the stream
Danube rolls in the moonbeam
Through rock-barriers : but she smiled
Never, she sat cold as salt :
Open-mouthed as a young child
Wondering with a mind at fault.
    Make the bed for Attila !

VII

Under the thin hoop of gold
Whence in waves her hair outrolled,
'Twixt her brows the women saw
Shadows of a vulture's claw
Gript in flight : strange knots that sped
Closing and dissolving aye :
Such as wicked dreams betray
When pale dawn creeps o'er the bed.
They might show the common pang
Known to virgins, in whom dread
Hunts their bliss like famished hounds ;
While the chiefs with roaring rounds
Tossed her to her lord, and sang
Praise of him whose hand was large,
Cheers for beauty brought to yield,
Chirrups of the trot afield,
Hurrahs of the battle-charge.

VIII

Those rock-faces hung with weed
Reddened : their great days of speed,
Slaughter, triumph, flood and flame,
Like a jealous frenzy wrought,
Scoffed at them and did them shame,
Quaffing idle, conquering naught.
O for the time when God decreed
      Earth the prey of Attila !
God called on thee in his wrath,
Trample it to mire ! 'Twas done.
Swift as Danube clove our path
Down from East to Western sun.
Huns ! behold your pasture, gaze,
Take, our king said : heel to flank
(Whisper it, the warhorse neighs !)
Forth we drove, and blood we drank
Fresh as dawn-dew : earth was ours :
Men were flocks we lashed and spurned :
Fast as windy flame devours,
Flame along the wind, we burned.
Arrow, javelin, spear, and sword !
Here the snows and there the plains ;
On ! our signal : onward poured
Torrents of the tightened reins,
Foaming over vine and corn
Hot against the city-wall.
Whisper it, you sound a horn
To the grey beast in the stall !
Yea, he whinnies at a nod.
O for sound of the trumpet-notes !
O for the time when, thunder-shod,
He that scarce can munch his oats
Hung on the peaks, brooded aloof,
Champed the grain of the wrath of God,
Pressed a cloud on the cowering roof,
Snorted out of the blackness fire !
Scarlet broke the sky, and down,
Hammering West with print of his hoof,
He burst out of the bosom of ire

Sharp as eyelight under thy frown,
    Attila, my Attila !

IX

Ravaged cities rolling smoke
Thick on cornfields dry and black
Wave his banners, bear his yoke.
Track the lightning, and you track
Attila. They moan : 'tis he !
Bleed : 'tis he ! Beneath his foot
Leagues are deserts charred and mute ;
Where he passed, there passed a sea.
    Attila, my Attila !

X

—Who breathed on the king cold breath ?
Said a voice amid the host,
He is Death that weds a ghost,
Else a ghost that weds with Death ?
Ildico's chill little hand
Shuddering he beheld : austere
Stared, as one who would command
Sight of what has filled his ear :
Plucked his thin beard, laughed disdain.
Feast, ye Huns ! His arm he raised,
Like the warrior, battle-dazed,
Joining to the fight amain.
    Make the bed for Attila !

XI

Silent Ildico stood up.
King and chief to pledge her well
Shocked sword sword and cup on cup,
Clamouring like a brazen bell.
Silent stepped the queenly slave.
Fair, by heaven ! she was to meet
On a midnight, near a grave,
Flapping wide the winding-sheet.

XII

Death and she walked through the crowd,
Out beyond the flush of light.
Ceremonious women bowed
Following her : 'twas middle night.
Then the warriors each on each
Spied, nor overloudly laughed ;
Like the victims of the leech,
Who have drunk of a strange draught.

XIII

Attila remained. Even so
Frowned he when he struck the blow,
Brained his horse that stumbled twice,
On a bloody day in Gaul,
Bellowing, Perish omens ! All
Marvelled at the sacrifice,
But the battle, swinging dim,
Rang off that axe-blow for him.
Attila, my Attila !

XIV

Brightening over Danube wheeled
Star by star ; and she, most fair,
Sweet as victory half-revealed,
Seized to make him glad and young ;
She, O sweet as the dark sign
Given him oft in battles gone,
When the voice within said, Dare !
And the trumpet-notes were sprung
Rapturous for the charge in line :
She lay waiting : fair as dawn
Wrapped in folds of night she lay ;
Secret, lustrous ; flaglike there,
Waiting him to stream and ray,
With one loosening blush outflung,
Colours of his hordes of horse
Ranked for combat : still he hung
Like the fever-dreading air,
Cursed of heat ; and as a corse

I

Gathers vultures, in his brain
Images of her eyes and kiss
Plucked at the limbs that could remain
Loitering nigh the doors of bliss.
     Make the bed for Attila !

                    XV

Passion on one hand, on one
Destiny led forth the Hun.
Heard ye outcries of affright,
Voices that through many a fray,
In the press of flag and spear,
Warned the king of peril near ?
Men were dumb, they gave him way,
Eager heads to left and right,
Like the bearded standard, thrust,
As in battle, for a nod
From their lord of battle-dust.
     Attila, my Attila !
Slow between the lines he trod.
Saw ye not the sun drop slow
On this nuptial day, ere eve
Pierced him on the couch aglow ?
     Attila, my Attila !
Here and there his heart would cleave
Clotted memory for a space :
Some stout chief's familiar face,
Choicest of his fighting brood,
Touched him, as 'twere one to know
Ere he met his bride's embrace.
     Attila, my Attila !
Twisting fingers in a beard
Scant as winter underwood,
With a narrowed eye he peered ;
Like the sunset's graver red
Up old pine-stems. Grave he stood
Eyeing them on whom was shed
Burning light from him alone.
     Attila, my Attila !

Red were they whose mouths recalled
Where the slaughter mounted high,
High on it, o'er earth appalled,
He ; heaven's finger in their sight
Raising him on waves of dead ;
Up to heaven his trumpets blown.
O for the time when God's delight
  Crowned the head of Attila !
Hungry river of the crag
Stretching hands for earth he came :
Force and Speed astride his name
Pointed back to spear and flag.
He came out of miracle cloud,
Lightning-swift and spectre-lean.
Now those days are in a shroud :
Have him to his ghostly queen.
  Make the bed for Attila !

XVI

One, with winecups overstrung,
Cried him farewell in Rome's tongue.
Who ? for the great king turned as though
Wrath to the shaft's head strained the bow.
Nay, not wrath the king possessed,
But a radiance of the breast.
In that sound he had the key
Of his cunning malady.
Lo, where gleamed the sapphire lake,
Leo, with his Rome at stake,
Drew blank air to hues and forms ;
Whereof Two that shone distinct,[1]
Linked as orbed stars are linked,
Clear among the myriad swarms,
In a constellation, dashed
Full on horse and rider's eyes
Sunless light, but light it was—
Light that blinded and abashed,
Froze his members, bade him pause,
Caught him mid-gallop, blazed him home.
  Attila, my Attila !

What are streams that cease to flow ?
What was Attila, rolled thence,
Cheated by a juggler's show ?
Like that lake of blue intense,
Under tempest lashed to foam,
Lurid radiance, as he passed,
Filled him, and around was glassed,
When deep-voiced he uttered, Rome !

XVII

Rome ! the word was : and like meat
Flung to dogs the word was torn.
Soon Rome's magic priests shall bleat
Round their magic Pope forlorn !
Loud they swore the king had sworn
Vengeance on the Roman cheat,
Ere he passed as, grave and still,
Danube through the shouting hill :
Sworn it by his naked life !
Eagle, snakes these women are :
Take them on the wing ! but war,
Smoking war's the warrior's wife !
Then for plunder ! then for brides
Won without a winking priest !—
Danube whirled his train of tides
Black toward the yellow East.
      Make the bed for Attila !

XVIII

Chirrups of the trot afield,
Hurrahs of the battle-charge,
How they answered, how they pealed,
When the morning rose and drew
Bow and javelin, lance and targe,
In the nuptial casement's view !
      Attila, my Attila !
Down the hillspurs, out of tents
Glimmering in mid-forest, through
Mists of the cool morning scents,
Forth from city-alley, court,

Arch, the bounding horsemen flew,
Joined along the plains of dew,
Raced and gave the rein to sport,
Closed and streamed like curtain-rents
Fluttered by a wind, and flowed
Into squadrons : trumpets blew,
Chargers neighed, and trappings glowed
Brave as the bright Orient's.
Look on the seas that run to greet
Sunrise : look on the leagues of wheat :
Look on the lines and squares that fret
Leaping to level the lance blood-wet.
Tens of thousands, man and steed,
Tossing like field-flowers in Spring ;
Ready to be hurled at need
Whither their great lord may sling.
Finger Romeward, Romeward, King !
　　　Attila, my Attila !
Still the woman holds him fast
As a night-flag round the mast.

XIX

Nigh upon the fiery noon,
Out of ranks a roaring burst.
'Ware white women like the moon !
They are poison : they have thirst
First for love, and next for rule.
Jealous of the army, she ?
Ho, the little wanton fool !
We were his before she squealed
Blind for mother's milk, and heeled
Kicking on her mother's knee.
His in life and death are we :
She but one flower of a field.
We have given him bliss tenfold
In an hour to match her night :
　　　Attila, my Attila !
Still her arms the master hold,
As on wounds the scarf winds tight.

XX

Over Danube day no more,
Like the warrior's planted spear,
Stood to hail the King : in fear
Western day knocked at his door.
        Attila, my Attila !
Sudden in the army's eyes
Rolled a blast of lights and cries :
Flashing through them : Dead are ye !
Dead, ye Huns, and torn piecemeal !
See the ordered army reel
Stricken through the ribs : and see,
Wild for speed to cheat despair,
Horsemen, clutching knee to chin,
Crouch and dart they know not where.
        Attila, my Attila !
Faces covered, faces bare,
Light the palace-front like jets
Of a dreadful fire within.
Beating hands and driving hair
Start on roof and parapets.
Dust rolls up ; the slaughter din.
—Death to them who call him dead !
Death to them who doubt the tale !
Choking in his dusty veil,
Sank the sun on his death-bed.
        Make the bed for Attila !

XXI

'Tis the room where thunder sleeps.
Frenzy, as a wave to shore
Surging, burst the silent door,
And drew back to awful deeps,
Breath beaten out, foam-white. Anew
Howled and pressed the ghastly crew,
Like storm-waters over rocks.
        Attila, my Attila !
One long shaft of sunset red
Laid a finger on the bed.
Horror, with the snaky locks,
Shocked the surge to stiffened heaps,

Hoary as the glacier's head
Faced to the moon. Insane they look.
God it is in heaven who weeps
Fallen from his hand the Scourge he shook.
      Make the bed for Attila !

XXII

Square along the couch, and stark,
Like the sea-rejected thing
Sea-sucked white, behold their King.
      Attila, my Attila !
Beams that panted black and bright,
Scornful lightnings danced their sight :
Him they see an oak in bud,
Him an oaklog stripped of bark :
Him, their lord of day and night,
White, and lifting up his blood
Dumb for vengeance. Name us that,
Huddled in the corner dark,
Humped and grinning like a cat,
Teeth for lips !—'tis she ! she stares,
Glittering through her bristled hairs.
Rend her ! Pierce her to the hilt !
She is Murder : have her out !
What.! this little fist, as big
As the southern summer fig !
She is Madness, none may doubt.
Death, who dares deny her guilt !
Death, who says his blood she spilt !
      Make the bed for Attila !

XXIII

Torch and lamp and sunset-red
Fell three-fingered on the bed.
In the torch the beard-hair scant
With the great breast seemed to pant :
In the yellow lamp the limbs
Wavered, as the lake-flower swims :
In the sunset red the dead
Dead avowed him, dry blood-red.

XXIV

Hatred of that abject slave,
Earth, was in each chieftain's heart.
Earth has got him, whom God gave,
Earth may sing, and earth shall smart !
    Attila, my Attila !

XXV

Thus their prayer was raved and ceased.
Then had Vengeance of her feast
Scent in their quick pang to smite
Which they knew not, but huge pain
Urged them for some victim slain
Swift, and blotted from the sight.
Each at each, a crouching beast,
Glared, and quivered for the word.
Each at each, and all on that,
Humped and grinning like a cat,
Head-bound with its bridal-wreath.
Then the bitter chamber heard
Vengeance in a cauldron seethe.
Hurried counsel rage and craft
Yelped to hungry men, whose teeth
Hard the grey lip-ringlet gnawed,
Gleaming till their fury laughed.
With the steel-hilt in the clutch,
Eyes were shot on her that froze
In their blood-thirst overawed ;
Burned to rend, yet feared to touch.
She that was his nuptial rose,
She was of his heart's blood clad :
Oh ! the last of him she had !—
Could a little fist as big
As the southern summer fig
Push a dagger's point to pierce
Ribs like those ? Who else ! They glared
Each at each. Suspicion fierce
Many a black remembrance bared.
    Attila, my Attila !

Death, who dares deny her guilt !
Death, who says his blood she spilt !
Traitor he, who stands between !
Swift to hell, who harms the Queen !
She, the wild contention's cause,
Combed her hair with quiet paws.
      Make the bed for Attila !

XXVI

Night was on the host in arms.
Night, as never night before,
Hearkened to an army's roar
Breaking up in snaky swarms :
Torch and steel and snorting steed,
Hunted by the cry of blood,
Cursed with blindness, mad for day.
Where the torches ran a flood,
Tales of him and of the deed
Showered like a torrent spray.
Fear of silence made them strive
Loud in warrior-hymns that grew
Hoarse for slaughter yet unwreaked.
Ghostly Night across the hive
With a crimson finger drew
Letters on her breast and shrieked.
Night was on them like the mould
On the buried half alive.
Night, their bloody Queen, her fold
Wound on them and struck them through.
      Make the bed for Attila !

XXVII

Earth has got him whom God gave,
Earth may sing, and earth shall smart !
None of earth shall know his grave.
They that dig with Death depart.
      Attila, my Attila !

XXVIII

Thus their prayer was raved and passed :
Passed in peace their red sunset :
Hewn and earthed those men of sweat
Who had housed him in the vast,
Where no mortal might declare,
There lies he—his end was there !
    Attila, my Attila !

XXIX

Kingless was the army left :
Of its head the race bereft.
Every fury of the pit
Tortured and dismembered it.
Lo, upon a silent hour,
When the pitch of frost subsides,
Danube with a shout of power
Loosens his imprisoned tides :
Wide around the frighted plains
Shake to hear his riven chains,
Dreadfuller than heaven in wrath,
As he makes himself a path :
High leap the ice-cracks, towering pile
Floes to bergs, and giant peers
Wrestle on a drifted isle ;
Island on ice-island rears ;
Dissolution battles fast :
Big the senseless Titans loom,
Through a mist of common doom
Striving which shall die the last :
Till a gentle-breathing morn
Frees the stream from bank to bank
So the Empire built of scorn
Agonized, dissolved and sank.
Of the Queen no more was told
Than of leaf on Danube rolled.
    Make the bed for Attila !

MEN AND MAN *

I

MEN the Angels eyed ;
And here they were wild waves,
And there as marsh descried ;
Men the Angels eyed,
And liked the picture best
Where they were greenly dressed
In brotherhood of graves.

II

Man the Angels marked :
He led a host through murk,
On fearful seas embarked ;
Man the Angels marked ;
To think without a nay,
That he was good as they,
And help him at his work.

III

Man and Angels, ye
A sluggish fen shall drain,
Shall quell a warring sea.
Man and Angels, ye,
Whom stain of strife befouls,
A light to kindle souls
Bear radiant in the stain.

SEED-TIME *

I

FLOWERS of the willow-herb are wool ;
Flowers of the briar berries red ;
Speeding their seed as the breeze may rule,
Flowers of the thistle loosen the thread.
Flowers of the clematis drip in beard,
Slack from the fir-tree youngly climbed ;
Chaplets in air, flies foliage seared ;
Heeled upon earth, lie clusters rimed.

II

Where were skies of the mantle stained
Orange and scarlet, a coat of frieze
Travels from North till day has waned,
Tattered, soaked in the ditch's dyes ;
Tumbles the rook under grey or slate ;
Else, enfolding us, damps to the bone ;
Narrows the world to my neighbour's gate ;
Paints me Life as a wheezy crone.

III

Now seems none but the spider lord ;
Star in circle his web waits prey,
Silvering bush-mounds, blue brushing sward ;
Slow runs the hour, swift flits the ray.
Now to his thread-shroud is he nigh,
Nigh to the tangle where wings are sealed,
He who frolicked the jewelled fly ;
All is adroop on the down and the weald.

IV

Mists more lone for the sheep-bell enwrap
Nights that tardily let slip a morn
Paler than moons, and on noontide's lap
Flame dies cold, like the rose late born.
Rose born late, born withered in bud !—
I, even I, for a zenith of sun
Cry, to fulfil me, nourish my blood :
O for a day of the long light, one !

V

Master the blood, nor read by chills,
Earth admonishes : Hast thou ploughed,
Sown, reaped, harvested grain for the mills,
Thou hast the light over shadow of cloud.
Steadily eyeing, before that wail,
Animal-infant, thy mind began,
Momently nearer me : should sight fail,
Plod in the track of the husbandman.[1]

VI

Verily now is our season of seed,
Now in our Autumn ; and Earth discerns
Them that have served her in them that can read,
Glassing, where under the surface she burns,
Quick at her wheel, while the fuel, decay,
Brightens the fire of renewal : and we ?
Death is the word of a bovine day,
Know you the breast of the springing To-be.

HARD WEATHER

Bursts from a rending East in flaws
The young green leaflet's harrier, sworn
To strew the garden, strip the shaws,
And show our Spring with banner torn.
Was ever such virago morn ?
The wind has teeth, the wind has claws.
All the wind's wolves through woods are loose,
The wild wind's falconry aloft.
Shrill underfoot the grassblade shrews,
At gallop, clumped, and down the croft
Bestrid by shadows, beaten, tossed ;
It seems a scythe, it seems a rod.
The howl is up at the howl's accost ;
The shivers greet and the shivers nod.
Is the land ship ? we are rolled, we drive
Tritonly, cleaving hiss and hum ;
Whirl with the dead, or mount or dive,
Or down in dregs, or on in scum.
And drums the distant, pipes the near,
And vale and hill are grey in grey,
As when the surge is crumbling sheer,
And sea-mews wing the haze of spray.
Clouds—are they bony witches ?—swarms,
Darting swift on the robber's flight,
Hurry an infant sky in arms :
It peeps, it becks ; 'tis day, 'tis night.

Black while over the loop of blue
The swathe is closed, like shroud on corse.
Lo, as if swift the Furies flew,
The Fates at heel at a cry to horse !

Interpret me the savage whirr :
And is it Nature scourged, or she,
Her offspring's executioner,
Reducing land to barren sea ?
But is there meaning in a day
When this fierce angel of the air,
Intent to throw, and haply slay,
Can for what breath of life we bear
Exact the wrestle ? Call to mind
The many meanings glistening up
When Nature, to her nurslings kind,
Hands them the fruitage and the cup !
And seek we rich significance
Not otherwhere than with those tides
Of pleasure on the sunned expanse,
Whose flow deludes, whose ebb derides ?

Look in the face of men who fare
Lock-mouthed, a match in lungs and thews
For this fierce angel of the air,
To twist with him and take his bruise.
That is the face beloved of old
Of Earth, young mother of her brood :
Nor broken for us shows the mould
When muscle is in mind renewed :
Though farther from her nature rude,
Yet nearer to her spirit's hold :
And though of gentler mood serene,
Still forceful of her fountain-jet.
So shall her blows be shrewdly met,
Be luminously read the scene
Where Life is at her grindstone set,
That she may give us edgeing keen,
String us for battle, till as play
The common strokes of fortune shower.

Such meaning in a dagger-day
Our wits may clasp to wax in power.
Yea, feel us warmer at her breast,
By spin of blood in lusty drill,
Than when her honeyed hands caressed,
And Pleasure, sapping, seemed to fill.

Behold the life at ease ; it drifts.
The sharpened life commands its course.
She winnows, winnows roughly ; sifts,
To dip her chosen in her source :
Contention is the vital force,
Whence pluck they brain, her prize of gifts,
Sky of the senses ! on which height,
Not disconnected, yet released,
They see how spirit comes to light,
Through conquest of the inner beast,
Which Measure tames to movement sane,
In harmony with what is fair.
Never is Earth misread by brain :
That is the welling of her, there
The mirror : with one step beyond,
For likewise is it voice ; and more,
Benignest kinship bids respond,
When wail the weak, and them restore
Whom days as fell as this may rive,
While Earth sits ebon in her gloom,
Us atomies of life alive
Unheeding, bent on life to come.
Her children of the labouring brain,
These are the champions of the race,
True parents, and the sole humane,
With understanding for their base.
Earth yields the milk, but all her mind
Is vowed to thresh for stouter stock.
Her passion for old giantkind,
That scaled the mount, uphurled the rock,
Devolves on them who read aright
Her meaning and devoutly serve ;
Nor in her starlessness of night
Peruse her with the craven nerve :

But even as she from grass to corn,
To eagle high from grubbing mole,
Prove in strong brain her noblest born,
The station for the flight of soul.

NIGHT OF FROST IN MAY *

WITH splendour of a silver day,
A frosted night had opened May :
And on that plumed and armoured night,
As one close temple hove our wood,
Its border leafage virgin white.
Remote down air an owl hallooed.
The black twig dropped without a twirl ;
The bud in jewelled grasp was nipped ;
The brown leaf cracked a scorching curl ;
A crystal off the green leaf slipped.
Across the tracks of rimy tan,
Some busy thread at whiles would shoot ;
A limping minnow-rillet ran,
To hang upon an icy foot.

In this shrill hush of quietude,
The ear conceived a severing cry.[1]
Almost it let the sound elude,
When chuckles three, a warble shy,
From hazels of the garden came,
Near by the crimson-windowed farm.
They laid the trance on breath and frame,
A prelude of the passion-charm.

Then soon was heard, not sooner heard
Than answered, doubled, trebled, more,
Voice of an Eden in the bird
Renewing with his pipe of four
The sob : a troubled Eden, rich
In throb of heart : unnumbered throats
Flung upward at a fountain's pitch
The fervour of the four long notes,

That on the fountain's pool subside,
Exult and ruffle and upspring :
Endless the crossing multiplied
Of silver and of golden string.
There chimed a bubbled underbrew
With witch-wild spray of vocal dew.

It seemed a single harper swept
Our wild wood's inner chords and waked
A spirit that for yearning ached
Ere men desired and joyed or wept.
Or now a legion ravishing
Musician rivals did unite
In love of sweetness high to sing
The subtle song that rivals light ;
From breast of earth to breast of sky :
And they were secret, they were nigh :
A hand the magic might disperse ;
The magic swung my universe.

Yet sharpened breath forbade to dream,
Where all was visionary gleam ;
Where Seasons, as with cymbals, clashed ;
And feelings, passing joy and woe,
Churned, gurgled, spouted, interflashed,
Nor either was the one we know :
Nor pregnant of the heart contained
In us were they, that griefless plained,
That plaining soared ; and through the heart
Struck to one note the wide apart :—
A passion surgent from despair ;
A paining bliss in fervid cold ;
Off the last vital edge of air,
Leap heavenward of the lofty-souled,
For rapture of a wine of tears ;
As had a star among the spheres
Caught up our earth to some mid-height
Of double life to ear and sight,
She giving voice to thought that shines
Keen-brilliant of her deepest mines ;
While steely drips the rillet clinked,
And hoar with crust the cowslip swelled.

K

Then was the lyre of earth beheld,
Then heard by me : it holds me linked ;
Across the years to dead-ebb shores
I stand on, my blood-thrill restores.
But would I conjure into me
Those issue notes, I must review
What serious breath the woodland drew ;
The low throb of expectancy ;
How the white mother-muteness pressed
On leaf and meadow-herb ; how shook,
Nigh speech of mouth, the sparkle-crest
Seen spinning on the bracken-crook.

THE THRUSH IN FEBRUARY *

I KNOW him, February's thrush,
And loud at eve he valentines
On sprays that paw the naked bush
Where soon will sprout the thorns and bines.

Now ere the foreign singer thrills
Our vale his plain-song pipe he pours,
A herald of the million bills ;
And heed him not, the loss is yours.

My study, flanked with ivied fir
And budded beech with dry leaves curled,
Perched over yew and juniper,
He neighbours, piping to his world :—

The wooded pathways dank on brown,
The branches on grey cloud a web,
The long green roller of the down,
An image of the deluge-ebb :—

And farther, they may hear along
The stream beneath the poplar row.
By fits, like welling rocks, the song
Spouts of a blushful Spring in flow.

But most he loves to front the vale
When waves of warm South-western rains
Have left our heavens clear in pale,
With faintest beck of moist red veins :

Vermilion wings, by distance held
To pause aflight while fleeting swift :
And high aloft the pearl inshelled [1]
Her lucid glow in glow will lift ;

A little south of coloured sky ;
Directing, gravely amorous,
The human of a tender eye
Through pure celestial on us :

Remote, not alien ; still, not cold ;
Unraying yet, more pearl than star ;
She seems a while the vale to hold
In trance, and homelier makes the far.

Then Earth her sweet unscented breathes ;
An orb of lustre quits the height ;
And like broad iris-flags, in wreaths
The sky takes darkness, long ere quite.

His [2] Island voice then shall you hear,
Nor ever after separate
From such a twilight of the year
Advancing to the vernal gate.

He sings me, out of Winter's throat,
The young time with the life ahead ;
And my young time his leaping note
Recalls to spirit-mirth from dead.

Imbedded in a land of greed,
Of mammon-quakings dire as Earth's,
My care was but to soothe my need ;
At peace among the littleworths.

To light and song my yearning aimed ;
To that deep breast of song and light [3]
Which men have barrenest proclaimed ;
As 'tis to senses pricked with fright.

So mine are these new fruitings rich
The simple to the common brings ;
I keep the youth of souls who pitch
Their joy in this old heart of things :

Who feel the Coming young as aye,
Thrice hopeful on the ground we plough ;
Alive for life, awake to die ;
One voice to cheer the seedling Now.

Full lasting is the song, though he,
The singer, passes : lasting too,
For souls not lent in usury,
The rapture of the forward view.

With that I bear my senses fraught
Till what I am fast shoreward drives.
They are the vessel of the Thought.
The vessel splits, the Thought survives.

Nought else are we when sailing brave,
Save husks to raise and bid it burn.
Glimpse of its livingness will wave
A light the senses can discern

Across the river of the death,
Their close. Meanwhile, O twilight bird
Of promise ! bird of happy breath !
I hear, I would the City heard.

The City of the smoky fray ;
A prodded ox, it drags and moans :
Its Morrow no man's child ; its Day
A vulture's morsel beaked to bones.

It strives without a mark for strife ;
It feasts beside a famished host :
The loose restraint of wanton life,
That threatened penance in the ghost !

Yet there our battle urges ; there
Spring heroes many : issuing thence,
Names that should leave no vacant air
For fresh delight in confidence.

Life was to them the bag of grain,
And Death the weedy harrow's tooth.
Those warriors of the sighting brain
Give worn Humanity new youth.

Our song and star are they to lead
The tidal multitude and blind
From bestial to the higher breed
By fighting souls of love divined.

They scorned the ventral dream of peace,
Unknown in nature. This they knew :
That life begets with fair increase
Beyond the flesh, if life be true.

Just reason based on valiant blood
The instinct bred afield would match
To pipe thereof a swelling flood,
Were men of Earth made wise in watch.[4]

Though now the numbers count as drops
An urn might bear, they father Time.[5]
She shapes anew her dusty crops ;
Her quick in their own likeness climb.

Of their own force do they create ;
They climb to light, in her their root.
Your brutish cry at muffled fate
She smites with pangs of worse than brute.

She, judged of shrinking nerves, appears
A Mother whom no cry can melt ;
But read her past desires and fears,
The letters on her breast are spelt.

A slayer, yea, as when she pressed
Her savage to the slaughter-heaps,
To sacrifice she prompts her best :
She reaps them as the sower reaps.

But read her thought to speed the race,
And stars rush forth of blackest night ;
You chill not at a cold embrace
To come, nor dread a dubious might.

Her double visage, double voice,
In oneness rise to quench the doubt.
This breath, her gift, has only choice
Of service, breathe we in or out.

Since Pain and Pleasure on each hand
Led our wild steps from slimy rock
To yonder sweeps of gardenland,
We breathe but to be sword or block.[6]

The sighting brain her good decree
Accepts ; obeys those guides, in faith,
By reason hourly fed, that she,
To some the clod, to some the wraith,

Is more, no mask : a flame, a stream.
Flame, stream, are we, in mid career
From torrent source, delirious dream,
To heaven-reflecting currents clear.

And why the sons of Strength have been
Her cherished offspring ever ; how
The Spirit served by her is seen
Through Law ; perusing love will show.

Love born of knowledge, love that gains
Vitality as Earth it mates,
The meaning of the Pleasures, Pains,
The Life, the Death, illuminates.

For love we Earth, then serve we all ;
Her mystic secret then is ours :
We fall, or view our treasures fall,
Unclouded, as beholds her flowers

Earth, from a night of frosty wreck,
Enrobed in morning's mounted fire,
When lowly, with a broken neck,
The crocus lays her cheek to mire.

EARTH AND A WEDDED WOMAN *

I

THE shepherd, with his eye on hazy South,
Has told of rain upon the fall of day.
But promise is there none for Susan's drouth,
That he will come, who keeps in dry delay.
The freshest of the village three years gone,
She hangs as the white field-rose hangs short-lived :
   And she and Earth are one
   In withering unrevived.
Rain ! O the glad refresher of the grain !
And welcome waterspouts, had we sweet rain !

II

Ah, what is Marriage, says each pouting maid,
When she who wedded with the soldier hides
At home as good as widowed in the shade,
A lighthouse to the girls that would be brides :
Nor dares to give a lad an ogle, nor
To dream of dancing, but must hang and moan,
   Her husband in the war,
   And she to lie alone.
Rain ! O the glad refresher of the grain !
And welcome waterspouts, had we sweet rain !

III

They have not known ; they are not in the stream ;
Light as the flying seed-ball is their play,
The silly maids ! and happy souls they seem ;
Yet Grief would not change fates with such as they.
They have not struck the roots which meet the fires
Beneath, and bind us fast with Earth, to know
   The strength of her desires,
   The sternness of her woe,
Rain ! O the glad refresher of the grain !
And welcome waterspouts, had we sweet rain !

IV

Now, shepherd, see thy word, where without shower
A borderless low blotting Westward spreads.
The hall-clock holds the valley on the hour ;
Across an inner chamber thunder treads :
The dead leaf trips, the tree-top swings, the floor
Of dust whirls, dropping lumped : near thunder speaks,
   And drives the dames to door,
    Their kerchiefs flapped at cheeks.
Rain ! O the glad refresher of the grain !
And welcome waterspouts of blessed rain !

V

Through night, with bedroom window wide for air,
Lay Susan tranced to hear all heaven descend :
And gurgling voices came of Earth, and rare,
Past flowerful, breathings, deeper than life's end,
From her heaved breast of sacred common mould ;
Whereby this lone-laid wife was moved to feel
   Unworded things and old
    To her pained heart appeal.
Rain ! O the glad refresher of the grain !
And down in deluges of blessed rain !

VI

At morn she stood to live for ear and sight,
Love sky or cloud, or rose or grasses drenched.
A lureful devil, that in glow-worm light
Set languor writhing all its folds, she quenched.
But she would muse when neighbours praised her face,
Her services, and staunchness to her mate :
   Knowing by some dim trace,
    The change might bear a date.
Rain ! O the glad refresher of the grain !
Thrice beauteous is our sunshine after rain !

MOTHER TO BABE *

I

FLECK of sky you are,
Dropped through branches dark,
    O my little one, mine !
Promise of the star,
Outpour of the lark ;
    Beam and song divine.

II

See this precious gift,
Steeping in new birth
    All my being, for sign
Earth to heaven can lift,
Heaven descend on earth,
    Both in one be mine !

III

Life in light you glass [1]
When you peep and coo,
    You, my little one, mine !
Brooklet chirps to grass,
Daisy looks in dew
    Up to dear sunshine.

WOODLAND PEACE

SWEET as Eden is the air,
    And Eden-sweet the ray.
No Paradise is lost for them
Who foot by branching root and stem,
And lightly with the woodland share
    The change of night and day.

Here all say,
We serve her, even as I :
We brood, we strive to sky,†
We gaze upon decay,
We wot of life through death,
How each feeds each we spy ;
And is a tangle round,
Are patient ; what is dumb
We question not, nor ask
The silent to give sound,
The hidden to unmask,
The distant to draw near.

And this the woodland saith :
I know not hope or fear ;
I take whate'er may come ;
I raise my head to aspects fair,
From foul I turn away.

Sweet as Eden is the air,
    And Eden-sweet the ray.

OUTER AND INNER

I

FROM twig to twig the spider weaves
    At noon his webbing fine.
So near to mute the zephyrs flute
    That only leaflets dance.
The sun draws out of hazel leaves
    A smell of woodland wine.
I wake a swarm to sudden storm
    At any step's advance.

† In the original version these three lines ran thus :—
        Here all things say
        'We know not,' even as I.
        'We brood, we strive to sky,' etc,

II

Along my path is bugloss blue,
The star with fruit in moss ;
The foxgloves drop from throat to top
A daily lesser bell.
The blackest shadow, nurse of dew,
Has orange skeins across ;
And keenly red is one thin thread
That flashing seems to swell.

III

My world I note ere fancy comes,
Minutest hushed observe :
What busy bits of motioned wits
Through antlered mosswork strive.
But now so low the stillness hums,
My springs of seeing swerve,
For half a wink to thrill and think
The woods with nymphs alive.

IV

I neighbour the invisible
So close that my consent
Is only asked for spirits masked
To leap from trees and flowers.
And this because with them I dwell
In thought, while calmly bent
To read the lines dear Earth designs
Shall speak her life on ours.

V

Accept, she says ; it is not hard
In woods ; but she in towns
Repeats, accept ; and have we wept,
And have we quailed with fears,
Or shrunk with horrors, sure reward
We have whom knowledge crowns ;
Who see in mould the rose unfold,
The soul through blood and tears.

NATURE AND LIFE *

I

LEAVE the uproar : at a leap
Thou shalt strike a woodland path,
Enter silence, not of sleep,
Under shadows, not of wrath ;
Breath which is the spirit's bath
In the old Beginnings find,
And endow them with a mind,
Seed for seedling, swathe for swathe.
That gives Nature to us, this
Give we her, and so we kiss.

II

Fruitful is it so : but hear
How within the shell thou art,
Music sounds ; nor other near
Can to such a tremor start.
Of the waves our life is part ;
They our running harvests bear :
Back to them for manful air,
Laden with the woodland's heart !
That gives Battle to us, this
Give we it, and good the kiss.

DIRGE IN WOODS

A WIND sways the pines,
        And below
Not a breath of wild air ;
Still as the mosses that glow
On the flooring and over the lines
Of the roots here and there.

The pine-tree drops its dead ;
They are quiet, as under the sea.
Overhead, overhead
Rushes life in a race,
As the clouds the clouds chase ;
      And we go,
And we drop like the fruits of the tree,
      Even we,
      Even so.

CHANGE IN RECURRENCE *

I

I STOOD at the gate of the cot
Where my darling, with side-glance demure,
Would spy, on her trim garden-plot,
The busy wild things chase and lure.
For these with their ways were her feast ;
They had surety no enemy lurked.
Their deftest of tricks to their least
She gathered in watch as she worked.

II

When berries were red on her ash,
The blackbird would rifle them rough,
Till the ground underneath looked a gash,
And her rogue grew the round of a chough.
The squirrel cocked ear o'er his hoop,
Up the spruce, quick as eye, trailing brush.
She knew any tit of the troop
All as well as the snail-tapping thrush.

III

I gazed : 'twas the scene of the frame,
With the face, the dear life for me, fled.
No window a lute to my name,
No watcher there plying the thread.
But the blackbird hung pecking at will ;
The squirrel from cone hopped to cone ;
The thrush had a snail in his bill,
And tap-tapped the shell hard on a stone.

HYMN TO COLOUR *

I

With Life and Death I walked when Love appeared,
And made them on each side a shadow seem.
Through wooded vales the land of dawn we neared,
Where down smooth rapids whirls the helmless dream
To fall on daylight ; and night puts away
      Her darker veil for grey.

II

In that grey veil green grassblades brushed we by ;
We came where woods breathed sharp, and overhead
Rocks raised clear horns on a transforming sky :
Around, save for those shapes, with him who led
And linked them, desert varied by no sign
      Of other life than mine.

III

By this the dark-winged planet, raying wide,
From the mild pearl-glow to the rose upborne,
Drew in his fires, less faint than far descried,
Pure-fronted on a stronger wave of morn :
And those two shapes the splendour interweaved
      Hung web-like, sank and heaved.

IV

Love took my hand when hidden stood the sun
To fling his robe on shoulder-heights of snow.
Then said : There lie they, Life and Death in one.
Whichever is, the other is : but know,
It is thy craving self that thou dost see,
      Not in them seeing me.

V

Shall man into the mystery of breath
From his quick beating pulse a pathway spy ?
Or learn the secret of the shrouded death,
By lifting up the lid of a white eye ?
Cleave thou thy way with fathering desire
      Of fire to reach to fire.

VI

Look now where Colour, the soul's bridegroom, makes
The house of heaven splendid for the bride.
To him as leaps a fountain she awakes,
In knotting arms, yet boundless : him beside,
She holds the flower to heaven, and by his power
      Brings heaven to the flower.

VII

He gives her homeliness in desert air,
And sovereignty in spaciousness ; he leads
Through widening chambers of surprise to where
Throbs rapture near an end that aye recedes,
Because his touch is infinite and lends
      A yonder to all ends.

VIII

Death begs of Life his blush ; Life Death persuades
To keep long day with his caresses graced.
He is the heart of light, the wing of shades,
The crown of beauty : never soul embraced
Of him can harbour unfaith ; soul of him
      Possessed walks never dim.

IX

Love eyed his rosy memories : he sang :
O bloom of dawn, breathed up from the gold sheaf
Held springing beneath Orient ! that dost hang
The space of dewdrops running over leaf ;
Thy fleetingness is bigger in the ghost
      Than Time with all his host !

X

Of thee to say behold, has said adieu :
But love remembers how the sky was green,
And how the grasses glimmered lightest blue ;
How saint-like grey took fervour : how the screen
Of cloud grew violet ; how thy moment came
      Between a blush and flame.

XI

Love saw the emissary eglantine
Break wave round thy white feet above the gloom ;
Lay finger on thy star ; thy raiment line
With cherub wing and limb ; wed thy soft bloom,
Gold-quivering like sunrays in thistle-down,
   Earth under rolling brown.

XII

They do not look through love to look on thee,
Grave heavenliness ! nor know they joy of sight,
Who deem the wave of rapt desire must be
Its wrecking and last issue of delight.
Dead seasons quicken in one petal-spot
   Of colour unforgot.

XIII

This way have men come out of brutishness
To spell the letters of the sky and read
A reflex upon earth else meaningless.
With thee, O fount of the Untimed ! to lead ;
Drink they of thee, thee eyeing, they unaged
   Shall on through brave wars waged.

XIV

More gardens will they win than any lost ;
The vile plucked out of them, the unlovely slain.
Not forfeiting the beast with which they are crossed,
To stature of the Gods will they attain.
They shall uplift their Earth to meet her Lord,
   Themselves the attuning chord !

XV

The song had ceased ; my vision with the song.
Then of those Shadows, which one made descent
Beside me I knew not : but Life ere long
Came on me in the public ways and bent
Eyes deeper than of old : Death met I too,
   And saw the dawn glow through.

WINTER HEAVENS

SHARP is the night, but stars with frost alive
Leap off the rim of earth across the dome.
It is a night to make the heavens our home
More than the nest whereto apace we strive.
Lengths down our road each fir-tree seems a hive,
In swarms outrushing from the golden comb.
They waken waves of thoughts that burst to foam :
The living throb in me, the dead revive.
Yon mantle clothes us : there, past mortal breath,
Life glistens on the river of the death.
It folds us, flesh and dust ; and have we knelt,
Or never knelt, or eyed as kine the springs
Of radiance, the radiance enrings :
And this is the soul's haven to have felt.

FRAGMENTS

LOVE is winged for two,
In the worst he weathers,
When their hearts are tied ;
But if they divide,
O too true !
Cracks a globe, and feathers, feathers,
Feathers all the ground bestrew.

I was breast of morning sea,
Rosy plume on forest dun,
I the laugh in rainy fleeces,
While with me
She made one.
Now must we pick up our pieces,
For that then so winged were we.

ASK, is Love divine,
Voices all are, ay.
Question for the sign,
There's a common sigh.

L

Would we, through our years,
Love forego,
Quit of scars and tears ?
Ah, but no, no, no !

Joy is fleet,
Sorrow slow.
Love, so sweet,
Sorrow will sow.
Love, that has flown
Ere day's decline,
Love to have known,
Sorrow, be mine !

THE LESSON OF GRIEF *

Not ere the bitter herb we taste,
Which ages thought of happy times,[1]
To plant us in a weeping waste,
Rings with our fellows this one heart
            Accordant chimes.

When I had shed my glad year's leaf,
I did believe I stood alone,
Till that great company of Grief
Taught me to know this craving heart
            For not my own.

WIND ON THE LYRE *

That was the chirp of Ariel
You heard, as overhead it flew,
The farther going more to dwell,
And wing our green to wed our blue ;
But whether note of joy or knell,
Not his own Father-singer knew ;
Nor yet can any mortal tell,
Save only how it shivers through ;
The breast of us a sounded shell,
The blood of us a lighted dew.

BREATH OF THE BRIAR

I

O BRIAR-SCENTS, on yon wet wing
Of warm South-west wind brushing by,
You mind me of the sweetest thing
That ever mingled frank and shy :
When she and I, by love enticed,
Beneath the orchard-apples met,
In equal halves a ripe one sliced,
And smelt the juices ere we ate.

II

That apple of the briar-scent,
Among our lost in Britain now,
Was green of rind, and redolent
Of sweetness as a milking cow.
The briar gives it back, well nigh
The damsel with her teeth on it ;
Her twinkle between frank and shy
My thirst to bite where she had bit.

TO J. M.

[JOHN MORLEY, 1867]

LET Fate or Insufficiency provide
Mean ends for men who what they are would be :
Penned in their narrow day no change they see
Save one which strikes the blow to brutes and pride.
Our faith is ours and comes not on a tide :
And whether Earth's great offspring, by decree,
Must rot if they abjure rapacity,
Not argument but effort shall decide.
They number many heads in that hard flock :
Trim swordsmen they push forth : yet try thy steel.
Thou, fighting for poor humankind, wilt feel
The strength of Roland in thy wrist to hew
A chasm sheer into the barrier rock,
And bring the army of the faithful through.

A CERTAIN PEOPLE

As Puritans they prominently wax,
And none more kindly gives and takes hard knocks.
Strong psalmic chanting, like to nasal cocks,
They join to thunderings of their hearty thwacks.
But naughtiness, with hoggery, not lacks
When Peace another door in them unlocks,
Where conscience shows the eyeing of an ox
Grown dully apprehensive of an Axe.
Graceless they are when gone to frivolousness,
Fearing the God they flout, the God they glut.
They need their pious exercises less
Than schooling in the Pleasures : fair belief
That these are devilish only to their thief,
Charged with an Axe nigh on the occiput.

TO COLONEL CHARLES *

I

An English heart, my commandant,
A soldier's eye you have, awake
To right and left ; with looks askant
On bulwarks not of adamant,
Where white our Channel waters break.

II

Where Grisnez winks at Dungeness
Across the ruffled strip of salt,
You look, and like the prospect less.
On men and guns would you lay stress,
To bid the Island's foemen halt.

III

While loud the Year is raising cry
At birth to know if it must bear
In history the bloody dye,
An English heart, a soldier's eye,
For the old country first will care.

IV

And how stands she, artillerist,
Among the vapours waxing dense,
With cannon charged ? 'Tis hist ! and hist !
And now she screws a gouty fist,
And now she counts to clutch her pence.

V

With shudders chill as aconite,
The couchant chewer of the cud
Will start at times in pussy fright
Before the dogs, when reads her sprite
The streaks predicting streams of blood.

VI

She thinks they may mean something ; thinks
They may mean nothing : haply both.
Where darkness all her daylight drinks,
She fain would find a leader lynx,
Not too much taxing mental sloth.

VII

Cleft like the fated house in twain,
One half is, Arm ! and one, Retrench !
Gambetta's word on dull MacMahon :
' The cow that sees a passing train ' :
So spies she Russian, German, French.

VIII

She ? no, her weakness : she unbraced
Among those athletes fronting storms !
The muscles less of steel than paste,
Why, they of nature feel distaste
For flash, much more for push, of arms.

IX

The poet sings, and well know we,
That ' iron draws men after it.'
But towering wealth may seem the tree
Which bears the fruit *Indemnity*,
And draw as fast as battle's fit,

X

If feeble be the hand on guard,
Alas, alas ! And nations are
Still the mad forces, though the scarred.
Should they once deem our emblem Pard
Wagger of tail for all save war ;—

XI

Mechanically screwed to flail
His flanks by Presses conjuring fear ;—
A money-bag with head and tail ;—
Too late may valour then avail !
As you beheld, my cannonier,

XII

When with the staff of Benedek,
On the plateau of Königgrätz,
You saw below that wedgeing speck ;
Foresaw proud Austria rammed to wreck,
Where Chlum drove deep in smoky jets.

February 1887.

ENGLAND BEFORE THE STORM

I

THE day that is the night of days,
With cannon-fire for sun ablaze,
We spy from any billow's lift ;
And England still this tidal drift !
Would she to sainted forethought vow
A space before the thunders flood,
That martyr of its hour might now
    Spare her the tears of blood.

II

Asleep upon her ancient deeds,
She hugs the vision plethora breeds,
And counts her manifold increase
Of treasure in the fruits of peace.
What curse on earth's improvident,
When the dread trumpet shatters rest,
Is wreaked, she knows, yet smiles content
    As cradle rocked from breast.

III

She, impious to the Lord of Hosts,
The valour of her offspring boasts,
Mindless that now on land and main
His heeded prayer is active brain.
No more great heart may guard the home,
Save eyed and armed and skilled to cleave
Yon swallower wave with shroud of foam,
    We see not distant heave.

IV

They stand to be her sacrifice,
The sons this mother flings like dice,
To face the odds and brave the Fates ;
As in those days of starry dates,
When cannon cannon's counterblast
Awakened, muzzle muzzle bowled,
And high in swathe of smoke the mast
    Its fighting rag outrolled.

1891.

TRAFALGAR DAY

He leads : we hear our Seaman's call
    In the roll of battles won ;
For he is Britain's Admiral
    Till setting of her sun.

When Britain's life was in her ships,
    He kept the sea as his own right ;
And saved us from more fell eclipse
    Than drops on day from blackest night.
Again his battle spat the flame !
    Again his victory flag men saw !
At sound of Nelson's chieftain name,
    A deeper breath did Freedom draw.

Each trusty captain knew his part :
    They served as men, not marshalled kine :
The pulses they of his great heart,
    With heads to work his main design.
Their Nelson's word, to beat the foe,
    And spare the fall'n, before them shone.
Good was the hour of blow for blow,
    And clear their course while they fought on.

Behold the Envied vanward sweep !—
    A day in mourning weeds adored !
Then Victory was wrought to weep ;
    Then sorrow crowned with laurel soared.
A breezeless flag above a shroud
    All Britain was when wind and wave,
To make her, passing human, proud,
    Brought his last gift from o'er the grave !

Uprose the soul of him a star
    On that brave day of Ocean days :
It rolled the smoke from Trafalgár
    To darken Austerlitz ablaze.
Are we the men of old, its light
    Will point us under every sky
The path he took ; and must we fight,
    Our Nelson be our battle-cry !

He leads : we hear our Seaman's call
    In the roll of battles won ;
For he is Britain's Admiral
    Till setting of her sun.

OCTOBER 21, 1905

THE hundred years have passed, and he
Whose name appeased a nation's fears,
As with a hand laid over sea ;
To thunder through the foeman's ears
Defeat before his blast of fire ;
Lives in the immortality
That poets dream and noblest souls desire.

Never did nation's need evoke
Hero like him for aid, the while
A continent was cannon-smoke
Or peace in slavery : this one Isle
Reflecting Nature : this one man
Her sea-hound and her mortal stroke,
With war-worn body aye in battle's van.

And do we love him well, as well
As he his country, we may greet,
With hand on steel, our passing bell
Nigh on the swing, for prelude sweet
To the music heard when his last breath
Hung on its ebb beside the knell,
And VICTORY in his ear sang gracious Death.

Ah, day of glory ! day of tears !
Day of a people bowed as one !
Behold across those hundred years
The lion flash of gun at gun :
Our bitter pride ; our love bereaved ;
What pall of cloud o'ercame our sun
That day, to bear his wreath, the end achieved.

Joy that no more with murder's frown
The ancient rivals bark apart.
Now Nelson to brave France is shown
A hero after her own heart :
And he now scanning that quick race,
To whom through life his glove was thrown,
Would know a sister spirit to embrace.

THE CALL *

UNDER what spell are we debased
 By fears for our inviolate Isle,
Whose record is of dangers faced
 And flung to heel with even smile ?
Is it a vaster force, a subtler guile ?

They say Exercitus designs
 To match the famed Salsipotent [1]
Where on her sceptre she reclines ;
 Awake : but were a slumber sent
By guilty gods, more fell his foul intent.

The subtler web, the vaster foe,
 Well may we meet when drilled for deeds :
But in these days of wealth at flow,
 A word of breezy warning breeds
The pained responses seen in lakeside reeds.

We fain would stand contemplative,
 All innocent as meadow grass ;
In human goodness fain believe,
 Believe a cloud is formed to pass ;
Its shadows chase with draughts of hippocras.

Others have gone : the way they went
 Sweet sunny now, and safe our nest.
Humanity, enlightenment,
 Against the warning hum protest :
Let the world hear that we know what is best.

So do the beatific speak ;
 Yet have they ears, and eyes as well ;
And if not with a paler cheek,
 They feel the shivers in them dwell,
That something of a dubious future tell.

For huge possessions render slack
 The power we need to hold them fast ;
Save when a quickened heart shall make
 Our people one, to meet what blast
May blow from temporal heavens overcast.

Our people one ! Nor they with strength
    Dependent on a single arm :
Alert, and braced the whole land's length,
    Rejoicing in their manhood's charm
For friend or foe ; to succour, not to harm.

Has ever weakness won esteem ?
    Or counts it as a prized ally ?
They who have read in History deem
    It ranks among the slavish fry,
Whose claim to live justiciary Fates deny.

It can not be declared we are
    A nation till from end to end
The land can show such front to war
    As bids a crouching foe expend
His ire in air, and preferably be friend.

We dreading him, we do him wrong ;
    For fears discolour, fears invite.
Like him, our task is to be strong ;
    Unlike him, claiming not by might
To snatch an envied treasure as a right.

So may a stouter brotherhood
    At home be signalled over sea
For righteous, and be understood,
    Nay, welcomed, when 'tis shown that we
All duties have embraced in being free.

This Britain slumbering, she is rich ;
    Lies placid as a cradled child ;
At times with an uneasy twitch,
    That tells of dreams unduly wild.
Shall she be with a foreign drug defiled ?

The grandeur of her deeds recall ;
    Look on her face so kindly fair :
This Britain ! and were she to fall,
    Mankind would breathe a harsher air,
The nations miss a light of leading rare.

1908.

FRANCE

DECEMBER 1870 *

I

WE look for her that sunlike stood
Upon the forehead of our day,
An orb of nations, radiating food
For body and for mind alway.
Where is the Shape of glad array ;
The nervous hands, the front of steel,
The clarion tongue ? Where is the bold proud face ?
We see a vacant place ;
We hear an iron heel.

II

O she that made the brave appeal
For manhood when our time was dark,[1]
And from our fetters drove the spark
Which was as lightning to reveal
New seasons, with the swifter play
Of pulses, and benigner day ;
She that divinely shook the dead
From living man ; that stretched ahead
Her resolute forefinger straight,
And marched toward the gloomy gate
Of earth's Untried, gave note, and in
The good name of Humanity
Called forth the daring vision ! she,
She likewise half corrupt of sin,
Angel and Wanton ! can it be ?
Her star has foundered in eclipse,
The shriek of madness on her lips ;
Shreds of her, and no more, we see.
There is horrible convulsion, smothered din,
As of one that in a grave-cloth struggles to be free.

III

Look not for spreading boughs
On the riven forest tree.
Look down where deep in blood and mire
Black thunder plants his feet and ploughs

The soil for ruin : that is France :
Still thrilling like a lyre,
Amazed to shivering discord from a fall
Sudden as that the lurid hosts recall
Who met in heaven the irreparable mischance.
O that is France !
The brilliant eyes to kindle bliss,
The shrewd quick lips to laugh and kiss,
Breasts that a sighing world inspire,
And laughter-dimpled countenance
Where soul and senses caught desire !

IV

Ever invoking fire from heaven, the fire
Has grasped her, unconsumable, but framed
For all the ecstasies of suffering dire.
Mother of Pride, her sanctuary shamed :
Mother of Delicacy, and made a mark
For outrage : Mother of Luxury, stripped stark :
Mother of Heroes, bondsmen : thro' the rains,
Across her boundaries, lo the league-long chains !
Fond Mother of her martial youth ; they pass,
Are spectres in her sight, are mown as grass !
Mother of Honour, and dishonoured : Mother
Of Glory, she condemned to crown with bays
Her victor, and be fountain of his praise.
Is there another curse ? There is another :
Compassionate her madness : is she not
Mother of Reason ? she that sees them mown
Like grass, her young ones ! Yea, in the low groan
And under the fixed thunder of this hour
Which holds the animate world in one foul blot
Tranced circumambient while relentless Power
Beaks at her heart and claws her limbs down-thrown,
She, with the plungeing lightnings overshot,
With madness for an armour against pain,
With milkless breasts for little ones athirst,
And round her all her noblest dying in vain,
Mother of Reason is she, trebly cursed,
To feel, to see, to justify the blow ;
Chamber to chamber of her sequent brain

Gives answer of the cause of her great woe,
Inexorably echoing thro' the vaults,
' 'Tis thus they reap in blood, in blood who sow :
' This is the sum of self-absolvëd faults.'
Doubt nor that thro' her grief, with sight supreme,
Thro' her delirium and despair's last dream,
Thro' pride, thro' bright illusion and the brood
Bewildering of her various Motherhood,
The high strong light within her, tho' she bleeds,
Traces the letters of returned misdeeds.
She sees what seed long sown, ripened of late,
Bears this fierce crop ; and she discerns her fate
From origin to agony, and on
As far as the wave washes long and wan
Off one disastrous impulse : for of waves
Our life is, and our deeds are pregnant graves
Blown rolling to the sunset from the dawn.

V

Ah, what a dawn of splendour, when her sowers [2]
Went forth and bent the necks of populations
And of their terrors and humiliations
Wove her the starry wreath that earthward lowers
Now in the figure of a burning yoke !
Her legions traversed North and South and East,
Of triumph they enjoyed the glutton's feast :
They grafted the green sprig, they lopped the oak.
They caught by the beard the tempests, by the scalp
The icy precipices, and clove sheer through
The heart of horror of the pinnacled Alp,
Emerging not as men whom mortals knew.
They were the earthquake and the hurricane,
The lightnings and the locusts, plagues of blight,
Plagues of the revel : they were Deluge rain,
And dreaded Conflagration ; lawless Might.
Death writes a reeling line along the snows,
Where under frozen mists they may be tracked,
Who men and elements provoked to foes,
And Gods : they were of god and beast compact :
Abhorred of all. Yet, how they sucked the teats

Of Carnage, thirsty issue of their dam,
Whose eagles, angrier than their oriflamme,
Flushed the vext earth with blood, green earth forgets.
The gay young generations mask her grief ;
Where bled her children hangs the loaded sheaf.
Forgetful is green earth ; the Gods alone
Remember everlastingly : they strike
Remorselessly, and ever like for like.
By their great memories the Gods are known.

VI

They are with her now, and in her ears, and known.
'Tis they that cast her to the dust for Strength,
Their slave, to feed on her fair body's length,
That once the sweetest and the proudest shone ;
Scoring for hideous dismemberment
Her limbs, as were the anguish-taking breath
Gone out of her in the insufferable descent
From her high chieftainship ; as were she death,
Who hears a voice of justice, feels the knife
Of torture, drinks all ignominy of life.
They are with her, and the painful Gods might weep,
If ever rain of tears came out of heaven
To flatter Weakness and bid conscience sleep,
Viewing the woe of this Immortal, driven
For the soul's life to drain the maddening cup
Of her own children's blood implacably :
Unsparing even as they to furrow up
The yellow land to likeness of a sea :
The bountiful fair land of vine and grain,
Of wit and grace and ardour, and strong roots,
Fruits perishable, imperishable fruits ;
Furrowed to likeness of the dim grey main
Behind the black obliterating cyclone.

VII

Behold, the Gods are with her, and are known.
Whom they abandon misery persecutes
No more : them half-eyed apathy may loan
The happiness of pitiable brutes.

Whom the just Gods abandon have no light,
No ruthless light of introspective eyes
That in the midst of misery scrutinize
The heart and its iniquities outright.
They rest, they smile and rest ; have earned perchance
Of ancient service quiet for a term ;
Quiet of old men dropping to the worm ;
And so goes out the soul. But not of France.
She cries for grief, and to the Gods she cries,
For fearfully their loosened hands chastise,
And icily they watch the rod's caress
Ravage her flesh from scourges merciless,
But she, inveterate of brain, discerns
That Pity has as little place as Joy
Among their roll of gifts ; for Strength she yearns.
For Strength, her idol once, too long her toy.
Lo, Strength is of the plain root-Virtues born :
Strength shall ye gain by service, prove in scorn,
Train by endurance, by devotion shape.
Strength is not won by miracle or rape.
It is the offspring of the modest years,
The gift of sire to son, thro' those firm laws
Which we name Gods ; which are the righteous cause,
The cause of man, and manhood's ministers.
Could France accept the fables of her priests,[3]
Who blest her banners in this game of beasts,
And now bid hope that heaven will intercede
To violate its laws in her sore need,
She would find comfort in her opiates :
Mother of Reason ! can she cheat the Fates ?
Would she, the champion of the open mind,
The Omnipotent's prime gift—the gift of growth—
Consent even for a night-time to be blind,
And sink her soul on the delusive sloth,
For fruits ethereal and material, both,
In peril of her place among mankind ?
The Mother of the many Laughters might
Call one poor shade of laughter in the light
Of her unwavering lamp to mark what things
The world puts faith in, careless of the truth :
What silly puppet-bodies danced on strings,

Attached by credence, we appear in sooth,
Demanding intercession, direct aid,
When the whole tragic tale hangs on a broken blade !

She swung the sword for centuries ; in a day
It slipped her, like a stream cut off from source.
She struck a feeble hand, and tried to pray,
Clamoured of treachery, and had recourse
To drunken outcries in her dream that Force
Needed but hear her shouting to obey.
Was she not formed to conquer ? The bright plumes
Of crested vanity shed graceful nods :
Transcendent in her foundries, Arts and looms,
Had France to fear the vengeance of the Gods ?
Her faith was on her battle-roll of names
Sheathed in the records of old war ; with dance
And song she thrilled her warriors and her dames,
Embracing her Dishonour : [4] gave him France
From head to foot, France present and to come,
So she might hear the trumpet and the drum—
Bellona and Bacchante ! rushing forth
On yon stout marching Schoolmen of the North.

Inveterate of brain, well knows she why
Strength failed her, faithful to himself the first :
Her dream is done, and she can read the sky,
And she can take into her heart the worst
Calamity to drug the shameful thought
Of days that made her as the man she served
A name of terror, but a thing unnerved :
Buying the trickster, by the trickster bought,
She for dominion, he to patch a throne.

VIII

Henceforth of her the Gods are known,
Open to them her breast is laid.
Inveterate of brain, heart-valiant,
Never did fairer creature pant
Before the altar and the blade !

M

IX

Swift fall the blows, and men upbraid,
And friends give echo blunt and cold,
The echo of the forest to the axe.
Within her are the fires that wax
For resurrection from the mould.

X

She snatched at heaven's flame of old,
And kindled nations : she was weak :
Frail sister of her heroic prototype,
The Man ; for sacrifice unripe,
She too must fill a Vulture's beak.
Deride the vanquished, and acclaim
The conqueror, who stains her fame,
Still the Gods love her, for that of high aim
Is this good France, the bleeding thing they stripe.

XI

She shall rise worthier of her prototype
Thro' her abasement deep ; the pain that runs
From nerve to nerve some victory achieves.
They lie like circle-strewn soaked Autumn-leaves
Which stain the forest scarlet, her fair sons !
And of their death her life is : of their blood
From many streams now urging to a flood,
No more divided, France shall rise afresh.
Of them she learns the lesson of the flesh :—
The lesson writ in red since first Time ran,
A hunter hunting down the beast in man :
That till the chasing out of its last vice,
The flesh was fashioned but for sacrifice.

Immortal Mother of a mortal host !
Thou suffering of the wounds that will not slay,
Wounds that bring death but take not life away !—
Stand fast and hearken while thy victors boast :
Hearken, and loathe that music evermore.
Slip loose thy garments woven of pride and shame :

The torture lurks in them, with them the blame
Shall pass to leave thee purer than before.
Undo thy jewels, thinking whence they came,
For what, and of the abominable name
Of her who in imperial beauty wore.

O Mother of a fated fleeting host
Conceived in the past days of sin, and born
Heirs of disease and arrogance and scorn,
Surrender, yield the weight of thy great ghost,
Like wings on air, to what the heavens proclaim
With trumpets from the multitudinous mounds
Where peace has filled the hearing of thy sons :
Albeit a pang of dissolution rounds
Each new discernment of the undying ones,
Do thou stoop to these graves here scattered wide
Along thy fields, as sunless billows roll ;
These ashes have the lesson for the soul.
' Die to thy Vanity, and strain thy Pride,
' Strip off thy Luxury : that thou mayst live,
' Die to thyself,' they say, ' as we have died
' From dear existence and the foe forgive,
' Nor pray for aught save in our little space
' To warm good seed to greet the fair earth's face.'
O Mother ! take their counsel, and so shall
The broader world breathe in on this thy home,
Light clear for thee the counter-changing dome,
Strength give thee, like an ocean's vast expanse
Off mountain cliffs, the generations all,
Not whirling in their narrow rings of foam,
But as a river forward. Soaring France !
Now is Humanity on trial in thee :
Now mayst thou gather humankind in fee :
Now prove that Reason is a quenchless scroll ;
Make of calamity thine aureole,
And bleeding head us thro' the troubles of the sea.

THE VITAL CHOICE *

I

Or shall we run with Artemis
Or yield the breast to Aphrodite ?
Both are mighty ;
Both give bliss ;
Each can torture if derided ;
Each claims worship undivided,
In her wake would have us wallow.

II

Youth must offer on bent knees
Homage unto one or other ;
Earth, the mother,
This decrees ;
And unto the pallid Scyther
Either points us shun we either,
Shun or too devoutly follow.

WITH THE HUNTRESS *

Through the water-eye of night,
Midway between eve and dawn,
See the chase, the rout, the flight
In deep forest ; oread, faun,
Goat-foot, antlers laid on neck ;
Ravenous all the line for speed.
See yon wavy sparkle beck
Sign of the Virgin Lady's lead.
Down her course a serpent star
Coils and shatters at her heels ;
Peals the horn exulting, peals
Plaintive, is it near or far.
Huntress, arrowy to pursue,
In and out of woody glen,
Under cliffs that tear the blue
Over torrent, over fen,

She and forest, where she skims
Feathery, darken and relume :
Those are her white-lightning limbs
Cleaving loads of leafy gloom.
Mountains hear her and call back,
Shrewd with night : a frosty wail
Distant : her the emerald vale
Folds, and wonders in her track.
Now her retinue is lean,
Many rearward ; streams the chase
Eager forth of covert ; seen
One hot tide the rapturous race.
Quiver-charged and crescent-crowned,
Up on a flash the lighted mound
Leaps she, bow to shoulder, shaft
Strung to barb with archer's craft,
Legs like plaited lyre-chords, feet
Songs to see, past pitch of sweet.
Fearful swiftness they outrun,
Shaggy wildness, grey or dun,
Challenge, charge of tusks elude :
Theirs the dance to tame the rude ;
Beast, and beast in manhood tame,
Follow we their silver flame.
Pride of flesh from bondage free,
Reaping vigour of its waste,
Marks her servitors, and she
Sanctifies the unembraced.
Nought of perilous she recks ;
Valour clothes her open breast ;
Sweet beyond the thrill of sex ;
Hallowed by the sex confessed.
Huntress arrowy to pursue,
Colder she than sunless dew,
She, that breath of upper air ;
Ay, but never lyrist sang,
Draught of Bacchus never sprang
Blood the bliss of Gods to share,
High o'er sweep of eagle wings,
Like the run with her, when rings
Clear her rally, and her dart,

In the forest's cavern heart,
Tells of her victorious aim.
Then is pause and chatter, cheer,
Laughter at some satyr lame,
Looks upon the fallen deer,
Measuring his noble crest ;
Here a favourite in her train,
Foremost mid her nymphs, caressed ;
All applauded. Shall she reign
Worshipped ? O to be with her there !
She, that breath of nimble air,
Lifts the breast to giant power.
Maid and man, and man and maid,
Who each other would devour
Elsewhere, by the chase betrayed,
There are comrades, led by her,
Maid-preserver, man-maker.

SONG IN THE SONGLESS

THEY have no song, the sedges dry,
    And still they sing.
It is within my breast they sing,
    As I pass by.
Within my breast they touch a string,
    They wake a sigh.
There is but sound of sedges dry ;
    In me they sing.

THE BURDEN OF STRENGTH

IF that thou hast the gift of strength, then know
Thy part is to uplift the trodden low ;
Else in a giant's grasp until the end
A hopeless wrestler shall thy soul contend.

THE MAIN REGRET

[WRITTEN FOR ' THE CHARING CROSS ALBUM ']

I

SEEN, too clear and historic within us, our sins of omission
Frown when the Autumn days strip us all ruthlessly bare.
They of our mortal diseases find never healing physician ;
Errors they of the soul, past the one hope to repair.

II

Sunshine might we have been unto seed under soil, or have
scattered
Seed to ascendant suns brighter than any that shone.
Even the limp-legged beggar a sick desperado has flattered
Back to a half-sloughed life cheered by the mere human
tone.

FRAGMENTS OF THE ILIAD IN ENGLISH HEXAMETER VERSE

ILIAD, i. 149

THE INVECTIVE OF ACHILLES

' HEIGH me ! brazen of front, thou glutton for plunder, how
can one,
Servant here to thy mandates, heed thee among our Achaians,
Either the mission hie on or stoutly do fight with the foemen ?
I, not hither I fared on account of the spear-armèd Trojans,
Pledged to the combat ; they unto me have in nowise a harm
done ;
Never have they, of a truth, come lifting my horses or oxen ;
Never in deep-soiled Phthia, the nurser of heroes, my harvests
Ravaged, they ; for between us is numbered full many a
darksome

Mountain, ay, therewith too the stretch of the windy sea-
    waters.
O hugely shameless! thee did we follow to hearten thee,
    justice
Pluck from the Dardans for him, Menelaos, thee too, thou
    dog-eyed!
Whereof little thy thought is, nought whatever thou reckest.
Worse, it is thou whose threat 'tis to ravish my prize from
    me, portion
Won with much labour, the which my gift from the sons of
    Achaia.
Never, in sooth, have I known my prize equal thine when
    Achaians
Gave some flourishing populous Trojan town up to pillage.
Nay, sure, mine were the hands did most in the storm of the
    combat,
Yet when came peradventure share of the booty amongst us,
Bigger to thee went the prize, while I some small blessèd
    thing bore
Off to the ships, my share of reward for my toil in the blood-
    shed!
So now go I to Phthia, for better by much it beseems me
Homeward go with my beakèd ships now, and I hold not in
    prospect,
I being outraged, thou mayst gather here plunder and wealth-
    store.'

i. 225

' BIBBER besotted, with scowl of a cur, having heart of a
    deer, thou!
Never to join to thy warriors armed for the press of the
    conflict,
Never for ambush forth with the princeliest sons of Achaia
Dared thy soul, for to thee that thing would have looked as a
    death-stroke.
Sooth, more easy it seems, down the lengthened array of
    Achaians,
Snatch at the prize of the one whose voice has been lifted
    against thee.
Ravening king of the folk, for that thou hast thy rule over
    abjects;

Else, son of Atreus, now were this outrage on me thy last one.
Nay, but I tell thee, and I do swear a big oath on it likewise :
Yea, by the sceptre here, and it surely bears branches and
    leaf-buds
Never again, since first it was lopped from its trunk on the
    mountains,
No more sprouting ; for round it all clean has the sharp metal
    clipped off
Leaves and the bark ; ay, verily now do the sons of Achaia,
Guardian hands of the counsels of Zeus, pronouncing the
    judgement,
Hold it aloft ; so now unto thee shall the oath have its portent;
Loud will the cry for Achilles burst from the sons of Achaia
Throughout the army, and thou chafe powerless, though in an
    anguish,
How to give succour when vast crops down under man-slaying
    Hector
Tumble expiring ; and thou deep in thee shalt tear at thy
    heart-strings,
Rage-wrung, thou, that in nought thou didst honour the
    flower of Achaians.'

TO A FRIEND LOST

[TOM TAYLOR]

When I remember, friend, whom lost I call,
Because a man beloved is taken hence,
The tender humour and the fire of sense
In your good eyes ; how full of heart for all,
And chiefly for the weaker by the wall,
You bore that lamp of sane benevolence ;
Then see I round you Death his shadows dense
Divide, and at your feet his emblems fall.
For surely are you one with the white host,
Spirits, whose memory is our vital air,
Through the great love of Earth they had : lo, these,
Like beams that throw the path on tossing seas,
Can bid us feel we keep them in the ghost,
Partakers of a strife they joyed to share.

YOUTH IN AGE

[HIS LAST POEM. 1908]

ONCE I was part of the music I heard
  On the boughs or sweet between earth and sky,
  For joy of the beating of wings on high
My heart shot into the breast of the bird.

I hear it now and I see it fly,
  And a life in wrinkles again is stirred,
  My heart shoots into the breast of the bird,
As it will for sheer love till the last long sigh.

APPENDIX

LOVE IN THE VALLEY

[FIRST VERSION FROM 'POEMS,' 1851]

For final version see p. 81 above.

UNDER yonder beech-tree standing on the green sward,
  Couch'd with her arms behind her little head,
Her knees folded up, and her tresses on her bosom,
  Lies my young love sleeping in the shade.
Had I the heart to slide one arm beneath her !
  Press her dreaming lips as her waist I folded slow,
Waking on the instant she could not but embrace me—
  Ah ! would she hold me, and never let me go ?

Shy as the squirrel, and wayward as the swallow ;
  Swift as the swallow when athwart the western flood
Circleting the surface he meets his mirror'd winglets,—
  Is that dear one in her maiden bud.
Shy as the squirrel whose nest is in the pine tops ;
  Gentle—ah ! that she were jealous as the dove !
Full of all the wildness of the woodland creatures,
  Happy in herself is the maiden that I love !

What can have taught her distrust of all I tell her ?
  Can she truly doubt me when looking on my brows ?
Nature never teaches distrust of tender love-tales,
  What can have taught her distrust of all my vows ?
No, she does not doubt me ! on a dewy eve-tide
  Whispering together beneath the listening moon,
I pray'd till her cheek flush'd, implored till she faltered—
  Fluttered to my bosom—ah ! to fly away so soon !

When her mother tends her before the laughing mirror,
  Tying up her laces, looping up her hair,
Often she thinks—were this wild thing wedded,
  I should have more love, and much less care.

When her mother tends her before the bashful mirror,
  Loosening her laces, combing down her curls,
Often she thinks—were this wild thing wedded,
  I should lose but one for so many boys and girls.

Clambering roses peep into her chamber,
  Jasmine and woodbine, breathe sweet, sweet,
White-necked swallows twittering of Summer,
  Fill her with balm and nested peace from head to feet.
Ah ! will the rose-bough see her lying lonely,
  When the petals fall and fierce bloom is on the leaves ?
Will the Autumn garners see her still ungathered,
  When the fickle swallows forsake the weeping eaves ?

Comes a sudden question—should a strange hand pluck her!
  Oh ! what an anguish smites me at the thought,
Should some idle lordling bribe her mind with jewels !—
  Can such beauty ever thus be bought ?
Sometimes the huntsmen prancing down the valley
  Eye the village lasses, full of sprightly mirth ;
They see as I see, mine is the fairest !
  Would she were older and could read my worth !

Are there not sweet maidens if she still deny me ?
  Show the bridal Heavens but one bright star ?
Wherefore thus then do I chase a shadow,
  Clattering one note like a brown eve-jar ?
So I rhyme and reason till she darts before me—
  Thro' the milky meadows from flower to flower she flies,
Sunning her sweet palms to shade her dazzled eyelids
  From the golden love that looks too eager in her eyes.

When at dawn she wakens, and her fair face gazes
  Out on the weather thro' the window panes,
Beauteous she looks ! like a white water-lily
  Bursting out of bud on the rippled river plains.
When from bed she rises clothed from neck to ankle
  In her long nightgown, sweet as boughs of May,
Beauteous she looks ! like a tall garden lily
  Pure from the night and perfect for the day !

Happy, happy time, when the grey star twinkles
    Over the fields all fresh with bloomy dew ;
When the cold-cheeked dawn grows ruddy up the twilight,
    And the gold sun wakes, and weds her in the blue.
Then when my darling tempts the early breezes,
    She the only star that dies not with the dark !
Powerless to speak all the ardour of my passion
    I catch her little hand as we listen to the lark.

Shall the birds in vain then valentine their sweethearts,
    Season after season tell a fruitless tale ?
Will not the virgin listen to their voices,
    Take the honeyed meaning, wear the bridal veil ?
Fears she frost of winter, fears she the bare branches ?
    Waits she the garlands of spring for her dower ?
Is she a nightingale that will not be nested
    Till the April woodland has built her bridal bower ?

Then come merry April with all thy birds and beauties !
    With thy crescent brows and thy flowery, showery glee ;
With thy budding leafage and fresh green pastures ;
    And may thy lustrous crescent grow a honeymoon for
      me !
Come merry month of the cuckoo and the violet !
    Come weeping Loveliness in all thy blue delight !
Lo ! the nest is ready, let me not languish longer !
    Bring her to my arms on the first May night.

NOTES

THE PROMISE IN DISTURBANCE, p. 5.

The ' Promise in Disturbance ' is an introduction to ' Modern Love,' written many years after the poem itself. The ' primal thunder ' in line 2 is the thunder heard in heaven on the fall of Lucifer and his angels.

MODERN LOVE, pp. 5-27.

I. ' He ' and ' she ' are the husband and wife, who loved each other once, but whose love has long been dying. They are lying awake at midnight, side by side, but divided in heart. The years past are imagined (ll. 12-13) as forming a dreary calendar written by the hand of Regret on the wall facing them as they lie.

III. This is the first of the sonnets † in which the husband speaks in his own person—as ' I.' ' The man ' in line 1 (referred to in the rest of the sonnet as ' he ' or ' him ') is the other man, on whom the wife is beginning to look with favour.

IV, V. ' He ' is now again the husband. In V (l. 14) the ' eyes nurtured to be looked at ' instead of to look, are his wife's eyes, which fail to see how near he still is to loving her passionately.

VI. In the first two and last two lines of VI, the poet is speaking, but in all the middle part of the sonnet the husband is speaking in his own person. He calls himself a ' tender fool ' to believe any longer that she loves him. He says that love is not dead in her, but has been transferred by her to another object ; he knows this since he heard her passionate sobbing at midnight. He is tempted to fling at her the hardest of all names for a woman.

VII, VIII. The husband is speaking.

IX. The poet is speaking, and ' he ' is the husband. But in the last four lines of IX the husband speaks, and continues to do so from X to XLVIII inclusive.

X. This sonnet suggests the original cause of the division : when the first rush of their love-passion had calmed down, and other interests called to the husband, the wife resented his caring for anything save their lovers' selfishness à deux. She looked to him to be always her ' Fairy Prince,' bringing her nothing but the joys of love, rather than to become a comrade in work for the world. Cf. lines 7-8 of sonnet L and last.

XIII. The husband tries vainly to persuade himself that it is the law of Nature, and should be the law of mortal men, that everything, including love, has its season and must pass. In the second last line ' for ever ' is a noun and the subject of ' whirls,' to which ' life ' is the object.

XIV. In lines 6-8 we have the first mention of the ' Lady,' gold-haired and witty, with whom the husband seeks distraction later on (XXVII,

---

† Swinburne wrote of them as ' sonnets,' though they have sixteen lines each.

XXXI). His wife, ' Madam,' thinks that he is attracted by the ' Lady ' and is jealous. The husband says that if his wife tries to win him back to her while at the same time playing with the other man herself, he would feel for her a contempt that would kill his present suffering, ' the nobler agony.'

XV. He shows his wife two love-letters, one which she wrote to him in the old days, and one which she has written now to the other man.

XVIII. l. 11. Amphion was a legendary singer of Greece, who, like Orpheus, charmed the trees into movement. The tall dancing country lass seemed to the lad's fancy like an oak-tree moving to music.

XXVII. He seeks 'distraction' by philandering with the ' golden head' with ' wit in it ' (XIV and XXXI). This personage in the poem is always called ' Lady ' or ' my Lady,' while the wife is ' Madam.'

XXX. As the two preceding sonnets have shown, the husband is getting little satisfaction, save to his vanity, out of his new amour. This sonnet (XXX) opens with six noble lines on the triumph of Love over the fear of Death. But from line 9 to the end the husband's cynical mood finds expression : he says that Nature is a deceptive and cruel mother ; the young, in the purity and joy of their first love, seem to be her happiest children and close to her, but they do not know her, or realize that her law is that Love should be only for the day (cf. XIII). She teaches them by the torture of loss to live for the day only, and to study themselves scientifically as animals with animal desires.

XXXIII refers to Raphael's picture of the spruce and comfortable young archangel slaying the fiend. He looks ' too serene ' for hard fighting, like the young Roman dandies at the battle of Pharsalia. In the real struggle of men and devil, men become ' half serpent,' and it is lucky if the fiend grows half human.

XXXIV. His wife is drawing nearer to him once more, and makes advances towards an explanation. He freezes her with polite banter. It is his worst crime, and he soon pays the penalty (XXXV).

XXXVIII. He asks ' my Lady ' to give him an ideal love, the only alternative to mere carnal appetite—' vileness.' For, as to his wife, he can no longer even pity her, who slew the love that was between him and her, and who, now that it is dead, sentimentally prizes it. Therefore he insists on being allowed to love ' my Lady,' or he will degenerate into a mere sensualist.

XXXIX. ' My Lady ' has conceded his request of the previous sonnet. The silent moon, as exquisite as music, seems to him a symbol of his ' Lady,' and the sound of the moonlit stream like a song from her. Suddenly his wife appears with the other man.

XL. In a revulsion of feeling he has to ask himself whether he can be jealous of his wife while loving ' my Lady.' The shock of the scene in the wood has effected a change in his attitude towards his wife. The note of cynicism that marked the middle of the poem disappears entirely from the husband's soliloquies.

XLI. Husband and wife agree to forgive each other and renew their love, though not without misgivings that they are taking up ' a lifeless vow to rob a living passion.'

XLII, XLIII. The renewal of perfect love between husband and wife is impossible. They seek refuge from this truth in each other's arms ; but there the barren fact is all the more apparent.

Their kisses being 'unblest' by love, only serve to separate them. He learns this, and next morning wanders disconsolate by the seashore.

XLIV. ll. 7-10. Had she, in the early days of their division, only made him suffer and not estranged him, it might have been possible for him to meet her heart now with no shadow of hypocrisy in his own. Ll. 11-16 : as it is, she detects that his restored affection is more pity than love and will have none of it.

XLV. In the night of this misery, he remembers his dream of love with the 'Lady.' His wife discerns this, from the incident of the rose, and has an agonizing fit of jealousy.

XLVI. She seeks an interview with the other man, courteously interrupted by her husband. Before she can speak he assures her that he has no base suspicions.

XLVIII. After a real explanation, from which he vainly hoped that a settled relationship would emerge, his wife flies, with the quixotic desire to leave him free to return to his 'Lady.' He knows that such is her motive, but fears the world will attribute to her a worse one.

XLIX. In the last two sonnets of the sequence the poet speaks, and 'he' once more means the husband. He follows his wife and finds her by the sea. She thinks his love for her has returned, and allows herself to dream that their old mutual relations are restored. But she knows her own heart well enough to be aware that this is a dream, and to forestall the awakening she commits suicide—the 'strength' of the 'desperate weak.' (Meredith told the writer of these notes that he meant that she killed herself.)

THE PATRIOT ENGINEER, pp. 28-31.

The young poet and his companion, on a pleasure tour that takes them to the Alps, fall in with an English engineer, on board a Meuse steamer. He is returning home to England, having thrown up his employment in Hungary, out of disgust with the Austrian tyranny over the brave Magyar patriots, which he can no longer endure to witness in silence. The historical events referred to are those of 1849.

[1] The 'traitor' refers to Görgei, the general who effected the surrender of the Magyar army at Vilagós on Aug. 13, 1849. The 'two despots' were Russia and Austria. Their combined forces rendered the submission at Vilagós necessary in the eyes of Görgei, who was therefore long regarded as a traitor by his countrymen—unjustly, as Meredith himself thought in later years when he had read the history.

[2] Following on the surrender of Vilagós, the Austrians shot four and hanged nine of the surrendered Magyar generals.

[3] The Double-Head' is the two-headed Austrian eagle, the 'beastly Bird' of the next stanza.

N

LUCIFER IN STARLIGHT,' p. 38.

[1] The scars formerly received by Lucifer during ' the old revolt from Awe' were those of his battle with the angels and his fall through the regions of air with his rebel hosts.

THE STAR SIRIUS, p. 38.

[1] Earth's ' lord '=the sun.

GRACE AND LOVE, p. 40.

The ' two vases ' are (1) the literal vase in which the lady arranges the flowers, and (2) the cup of the lover's soul into which she pours the ' image of herself,' though unmindful that she is doing so. Her grace and his love ' unite,' even if the ' strange fates ' withhold from him the ' starry more' which would be realized if she rewarded his love with her own.

THE WORLD'S ADVANCE, p. 41.

[1] ' That figure on a flat ' : viz., just as spiritually the mind's ascent is in changing directions but always upwards (' spiral '), so historically the progress of the world is from side to side but always forwards (zig-zag). The ' memorable Lady ' who called ' our mind's ascent ' ' Spiral,' is presumably Mrs. Browning (or Aurora Leigh), for in *Aurora Leigh*, Bk. iv. l. 1151, we read :

> ' What is art
> But life upon the larger scale, the higher,
> When, graduating up in a spiral line
> Of still expanding and ascending gyres,
> It pushes toward the intense significance
> Of all things, hungry for the Infinite ?
> Art's life,—and where we live we suffer and toil.'

THE WOODS OF WESTERMAIN, pp. 43-54.

The woods of Westermain are the mysterious woods of Nature, whose spirit no man can interpret unless he enter the woods with courage and love. Nature turns horrible to those who fear or carp at her.

[1] In the dull, patient, primæval stare of cattle you can read the spirit of the prehistoric ages, before mind had developed ; when creation slowly evolved through years and hours that were uncounted ; when earth was a slimy ridge emerging out of the waters ; when heaven was merely a space through which were whirled the lumps of matter.

[2] ' She ' throughout this poem, as in so many others, means our Mother Earth (Nature), conceived as a spirit somehow present in the woods and the sky and wild animals, and in the body and mind of man. The fullest exposition of the theme will be found in the poem ' Earth and Man,' p. 90 above.

[3] ' The white Foam-born ' is Aphrodite, the Greek goddess of love and beauty, who rose first out of the sea. She, and the other gods of the classical pantheon, Phoebus, Diana (Phoebe) and Pan, may still

have their place, says the poet, in any true modern reading of Earth, because they were conceived from deep knowledge of nature.

⁴ The proper relation of men and women is discussed. If man plays the tyrant, and, to flatter his own pride, will not let the woman show and cultivate her mind, the woman grows trickster. Tragedies have come from this, and the relation of man and woman, as the poet says a few lines further down, becomes like a battle of tiger and snake. They may in this fashion people the world, but it will only be in ' snarling plight.'

⁵ The ' Dragon ' or ' Dragon-fowl ' is self, egoism. Savage and cruel as he is before he is tamed, it is an error to attempt to kill him. He must be constrained and set to sociable uses, when he will prove a servant of great power. But this is only possible by passing through a series of changes : so Change must not be feared.

⁶ ' The Fount and Lure o' the chase ' is Love : it is symbolized as a fount of ' water hued as wine.'

⁷ Even in the heart that is under the purifying and altruistic influence of Love, you may discern the semblance of the Dragon of Self, though reduced to his proper place and dimensions—just as according to old country tradition you may see the diminutive semblance of an oak in the section of a bracken stem.

⁸ She ' who food for all provides ' is Earth or Nature, who works through Death as well as through Life.

⁹ The ' Triad ' is ' blood, brain and spirit,' or the body, the mind, and the soul. The three must all work together for any great object, or there will be disaster. The mere athlete, the mere intellectual, the mere emotionalist are all astray. ' Glassing,' three lines below = ' reflecting,'

¹⁰ Those who have explored the depths of the meaning of Earth, can wield Life, ' the chisel, axe and sword.' And for them (continues the poet in the following couplets) Life shall hold prophetic dreams ; shall re-echo in itself an answer to its question as to what it is for ; shall thrill to be changed from the rampant dragon of egoism, and stamped for service to others ; and shall suggest something that shall always conquer the fear of death.

¹¹ Viz. : If with the brood of the monster Self, you doubt everything which Self's narrow orbit excludes, if you are of the stiff, etc. . . . if you hate at all, then you are lost in Westermain.

¹² ' One whose eyes are out ' is Death—the skeleton, Meredith told the writer of these notes.

THE DAY OF THE DAUGHTER OF HADES, pp. 55-70.

This tale of Callistes and Skiágeneia is the invention of the poet, based on the old myth of Pluto and Persephone. The scene is laid in the flowery vale of Enna in Sicily, whither Pluto (Hades), the god of death, had formerly come up in a chariot to carry off to his kingdom of Darkness the Maid of Enna—Persephone, the daughter of Demeter, the earth-goddess. Demeter cursed the scene of the rape, and the green valley withered. But now again it blooms at spring-time. And in the twilight before dawn Callistes goes out to wait for the sun to rise over the hills that surround the sacred valley and lake (11).

But before the colours of dawn wave in the sky their signal to the

colours of earth, the rock is rent and a chariot bursts out. It carries
Persephone, coming up from her kingdom of Darkness, to visit her
mother Demeter in the light of the sun. Such was the myth into which the
Greeks translated the yearly springing of the corn. Callistes thus chances
to witness the meeting of ' the Twain '—Demeter, the ' great Mother,'
' our Lady of the sheaves,' and her daughter Persephone, the ' Lily of
Hades,' the ' mate of the Rayless.' Persephone has brought from her
dim underworld a grave smile, a smile like Sleep that purifies us from our
cravings (III).

When the vision of ' the Twain ' has gone by, Callistes recovers his
senses and his memory, and sees standing near him a maiden who had
' slipped from the car ' (v). She is Skiágeneia, the shadow-born child of
Persephone and Pluto ; she is the *Daughter of Hades.*

The rest of the poem describes her ' day upon earth,' which she passes
in company with Callistes. Her first song to Helios, the sun-god, is
answered by a hollow roar from underground, like the voice of the
Hundred-headed Titan bound under Mount Aetna hard by : it is really
the voice of her father Pluto calling after her. She continues all day to
rejoice in the sight of the fecundity of earth (vi).

Finally her song of joy in all things, uttered from the mountain-top
(VIII), betrays her whereabouts to her father Pluto, who comes up in his
terrible chariot to fetch her. Day turns to night as in eclipse, while
Callistes and the maiden hurry down off the mountain, and stand shuddering by the shore of the lake of Enna (IX). The dark driver sees them,
and tears his way through the waters of the lake to seize her (x). Callistes
is left alone with her name and her cry in his ears (xi), to long for her
till he dies (XII).

The central thought of the poem is the strange link between Life and
Death in spite of their opposition. Just because Skiágeneia is born from
the Darkness as well as from the spirit of Spring, she, better than the
human children of Earth, can understand the secrets of Earth and Pan
(VII). She has an infinite thirst for life, blessing the fruitfulness of men
and shunning their wanton destructiveness as in war (VII) ; but she knows
she must return to the Darkness, and when she goes it is not without joy
in her heart as well as sorrow. She has made the most of her ' day upon
Earth,' instead of uselessly repining because it was so brief.

[1] (vi) The hair of the dying was cut for Persephone, by an ancient
Greek custom. ' The Beneficent,' mentioned a few lines before, is
Demeter. ' Both '=Demeter and Persephone.

[2] (ix) ' The Three '=Demeter, Persephone, and Pluto.

PHOEBUS WITH ADMETUS, pp. 74-77.

Phoebus Apollo, the sun-god, having slain the Cyclops, was sentenced
by Zeus to serve a mortal for one year. His arrival at the farm of ' the
master' Admetus is described in verse II. The water welcomes him
(III), and prosperity comes to the farm where he resides (IV). We are
then told of the arts and crafts which he taught mankind during this
sojourn—trapping beasts and shooting birds of prey (v), story-telling
and dancing (vi), woodland pharmacy and the music of the lyre (VII).
In the last verse the shepherds call on animate and inanimate nature, the

beasts of the farm and the branches in woodland and rocky stream, to remember the god who had been their fellow.

¹ Phoebus being the sun-god, the moon is his sister sphere. The farm-servants, when Phoebus has ceased to be one of them, remember how he played on his flute at evening, till the moon silvered and shone.

MELAMPUS, pp. 77-80.

The Greek legend that the physician Melampus obtained the power of understanding the language of birds, after his ears had been licked by some young snakes which he had preserved from death, is used to illustrate the proper relation of the highest human life to the life of animals and insects, and of nature in general. Melampus, as we are told in the first and last lines of the poem, has that love which adds wisdom and insight to simple affection, and so learns from nature a harmony of healing as profound as the harmony of song.

¹ The Pierides were the Nine Muses. They were the chorus of Phoebus Apollo (' his own chorus '), god of the sun, of poetry, and of music.

THE THREE SINGERS TO YOUNG BLOOD, pp. 87-88.

Three views of love. *First*, gentle young love, heedless of all but nature's promptings. *Secondly*, the warnings of worldly calculation. *Thirdly*, the irresistible cry of passion.

THE ORCHARD AND THE HEATH, pp. 89-90.

The contrast is between the farmer's children of the rich orchard land and the gypsy children encamped on the moor.

EARTH AND MAN, pp. 90-97.

¹ This poem (which contains the fullest expression of Meredith's doctrine of Earth our Mother and her relation to us), opens with the figure of Earth feeding her offspring Man at her breast.

² ' The Invisible ' is used throughout this poem (again in verses xx *et seq.*) to mean the supernatural God as conceived by superstition, by Man desiring to escape from and deny his Mother Earth (Nature).

³ Earth's ' cherishing of her best-endowed ' is the survival of the fittest, which, though it seems to Man a ' wanton's choice,' has yet proved the path of progress (xvi).

⁴ ' Her just Lord ' is the true God, whom Man can only attain to see when he has already understood his Mother Earth. This, says the poet, is the true conception of God, as opposed to the miracle-mongering ' Invisible ' of verses VIII and xx. Man must attain to the spiritual through the natural, not through the supernatural. Meredith again and again in his poems reverts to the idea of the ultimate attainment to God *through* Earth—of a marriage of earth and heaven—*e.g.* ' wing our green to wed our blue ' in ' Wind on the Lyre,' p. 148.

THE SONG OF THEODOLINDA, pp. 97-101.

Meredith's own note to this poem was—'The legend of the Iron Crown of Lombardy, formed of a nail of the true Cross by order of the devout Queen Theodolinda, is well known. In this dramatic song she is seen passing through one of the higher temptations of the believing Christian.' [The 'temptation,' presumably, was that of spiritual pride. When the nail is white hot in the fire, Theodolinda has it laid on her breast (VII-X), and then hammered into the Crown (XII-XIII) by 'brown-cowled' monks (III).]

THE YOUNG PRINCESS, pp. 101-108.

The 'laws of love' are those administered among the romantic chivalry of mediaeval Provence.

I

The 'Princess' feels love for none of the lords, though she is of gentle spirit. Duels are fought on her account.

II

At last Lord Dusiote, pretending to have been wounded to death in fighting for her honour, obtains her troth, which she gives him as to a dying man, in pity and gratitude.

III

Not daring to face her by daylight, he leaves the court. After a year he returns to claim her, when she is being married to another; but she treats him as if he were a ghost returning.

IV

At midnight in the garden Lord Dusiote's squire waits under the orange boughs for the return of his master, who has gone in to claim the Princess as his affianced bride. He returns—dead, borne on the shoulders of the other lords, who have made him 'a ghost' indeed.

MANFRED, p. 109.

Byron's play *Manfred* is here mocked for a piece of egoistic melancholy posed before the footlights. Manfred, successor of 'Childe' Harold, goes up Alpine heights to soliloquise there on his own superior inability to love either man or nature—but with one eye turned down at 'the world of spinsterdom and clergy,' whose shocked attention it is his object to concentrate on himself. It is here suggested that if Manfred had really climbed the Alps, 'shedding rascal sweat,' he would have felt better for the exercise when he reached the top. Spiritual indigestion is bred in cities, not on mountains.

HERNANI, p. 109.

In Victor Hugo's tragedy, Hernani wins his bride, to whom he had not a perfect right, on condition that he will kill himself whenever he hears the old gentleman, her former possessor, blow his horn. As might be expected in a romantic tragedy, the horn sounds at a highly inconvenient moment. The poet here laughs at the sentiment of the piece, but ends by pointing out its true moral—a serious one, but even so not quite divorced from the Comic Muse.

THE NUPTIALS OF ATTILA, pp. 110-124.

Attila the Hun is camped near the Danube, tired for a while of world-destruction. 'Scorn of conquest' fills him, and he turns to thoughts of love. 'The damsel Ildico' is his chosen bride. Her dumb horror of him is hinted, while his warriors dislike his strange effeminacy and clamour to be led to fresh conquests. Throughout the marriage feast the bride neither speaks nor smiles. At last Attila rises to go forth to the bridal chamber (xv), when some one cries out 'Vale' ('farewell') in the tongue of Rome, and he answers, with a look of 'lurid radiance,' *Rome* (xvi). The warriors shout with joy at this promise of fresh war on Rome (xvii). Next morning they surge round the bridal chamber shouting to be led against the City, but all day there is no sign of life from their king. Next day, at sunset, he is found dead on the marriage bed (xxi). The Huns do not know, any more than posterity knows, whether he died by Ildico's hand or by the bursting of a blood-vessel; Ildico is found speechless and mad in a corner of the room (xxii-xxv). They honour him in death by killing those who dug his grave, so that no man may know where he lies (xxvii-xxviii). The army of foolish savages breaks up in bewilderment, wrath, and mutual suspicion (xxix).

[1] (xvi) A few months before his fatal 'nuptials' beside the Danube, Attila had advanced on Rome, and been turned back by 'the pressing eloquence of (Pope) Leo, his majestic aspect, and sacerdotal robes,' and, as legend narrates, by 'the apparition of the two apostles St. Peter and St. Paul.'—Gibbon, chap. xxxv.

MEN AND MAN, p. 125.

In the first line, 'Men' is the object of the verb, and 'Angels' is the subject; similarly in the second verse, line 1, 'Man' is the object. The Angels do not admire the ways of 'Men' collectively, till they see them united in the peace of the churchyard. The individual 'Man' is the hero preferred.

SEED-TIME, pp. 125-127.

[1] In verse iv the poet has uttered a cry of longing to escape from the chill of autumn for a 'day of the long light' to nourish his blood. This lapse of faith in Nature merits the reproof in verse v. 'Animal-infant' is Earth's word of contempt for that 'wail' or for him who utters it; before uttering it he had, by 'steadily eyeing,' come daily into a closer relation with Earth. Animal-infant means undeveloped like an animal, *i.e.* one by whom Nature's methods are simply judged according to the physical comfort (or the reverse) which they produce at the moment.

Nature's direction to any one whose faith in her falters is to observe the husbandman, whose craft depends upon Nature's wise preparations for the future.

NIGHT OF FROST IN MAY, pp. 130-132.

[1] In the second stanza (beginning ' In this shrill hush ') and following stanzas the song of the nightingale is described. First one sings alone from hazels near the farm, and then a number from the woodland.

THE THRUSH IN FEBRUARY, pp. 132-136.

[1] The ' moist red veins ' and ' vermilion wings ' are the cirrus clouds at sunset. The ' pearl inshelled ' is the evening star—the subject of the following two stanzas—' she seems a while the vale to hold in trance.' Everywhere else in the poem, for instance in the last thirteen stanzas, ' she ' means ' Earth,' Mother Nature.

[2] ' *His* Island voice ' means the English voice of the thrush.

[3] ' That deep breast of song and light ' is Earth's.

[4] If modern men would patiently learn the secret of Earth, their intellect, based on courage, would match the primitive instincts, and so raise a swelling flood of song.

[5] Though scanty in numbers, the heroes are the fathers of the future.

[6] This and the former verse mean that Earth's double aspects of Pain and Pleasure, Life and Death, have but one aim : to make us active warriors of good—otherwise we can but serve as raw material for heroic life in others. In the following verse ' those guides ' mean Pain and Pleasure, nature's means of forcing men along the path of evolution to higher things.

EARTH AND A WEDDED WOMAN, pp. 137-138.

The spirit of Earth includes the spirit of endurance. Susan, a wife left lonely and sad (I, II), learns this on a night of summer rain after long drought, when the splendour of Earth's elemental forces are revealed to her (IV, V) ; thenceforth, her weakness is gone and her ' neighbours ' notice the ' change,' which she herself knows can be dated from the night of summer rain (VI).

MOTHER TO BABE, p. 139.

[1] ' Glass '=' reflect.' A reflection of the fundamental life of the world is seen, irradiated, in the baby.

NATURE AND LIFE, p. 142.

I. Nature in the woods can give man refreshment by making him feel the primitive elemental forces, the seed of all things. But man has something to give in return, namely mind. Nature can only be interpreted by his mind, which is thus in its turn the giver of seed.

II. Even so, there is more in man than can be developed by the woodland. He has tones in his own being (' the shell thou art ') of music that cannot awake (' start ') anything in the woods to an answering echo (' to such a tremor '). For this he must go back to the ' waves ' of ordinary life, and win the courage that comes from the human struggle when he takes back into it the peacefulness found in the woods.

CHANGE IN RECURRENCE, p. 143.

After the death of his second wife in 1885, the poet is in their cottage garden again, among the birds and animals which she loved to watch. It is the frame without the picture : no one now calls his name musically from the open window, sewing as she watches the garden. But the birds and animals are about their tasks and pastimes, diligent as ever.

HYMN TO COLOUR, pp. 144-146.

A dualism runs through the thought of this poem. Light, Darkness, and Colour answer respectively to Life, Death, and Love. Colour is to Light and Darkness as Love is to Life and Death.

i. The poet, walking between Death and Life, is met by Love in the pale 'land of dawn,' between night and day, where dreams are floating fast to wreck on daylight.

ii. The mist of twilight is still grey, but already the natural green of the grass is visible. The sky in this mountain land begins to change towards dawn. The 'shapes' are Life and Death linked by Love. They and the poet seem alone.

iii. The morning star, as it rises into the reddening sky, seems to shine from a mere remote distance as the dawn grows. Life and Death seem to hang aloft, suffused together, in the radiance of the dawn, as clouds sinking and heaving in mountain land.

iv. Love stays close beside the poet and points to the shapes of Life and Death in the sky, saying that they are counterparts of each other, and cannot exist separately from each other ; and if they are not seen to be servants of Love. it is because a man's own selfish cravings obscure his spiritual sight.

v. It is not by questionings, but by the life of noble action and emotion that a man will thrive. He cannot learn the secret of life from the throbbings of his pulse, or the secret of death by looking into the eye of a corpse. But he can raise his own 'inner light' and flame to meet the answering light and flame from heaven.

vi. Dawn rises and makes the dull day splendid (Colour is taken as a type of beauty,—the beauty that is full of spiritual significance). The soul, in the close yet boundless embrace of her bridegroom Colour, finds that the humblest flower and the highest heavens are alike splendid to the eye that can see.

viii. ' He ' means ' Colour '.

ix. The colours of Dawn fade too soon, but they live in ' rosy memories.' So when the precious moment is passed, Love sings this hymn of thanksgiving and recollection addressed to Colour.

x-xiv. In Love's ' song,' verses x-xi recall chiefly the visible beauties of the recent sunrise, while xii-xiv celebrate rather the spiritual significance of the Colour-moments of life.

xv. Love having ended his song to Colour, the vision is over ; but when the poet next sees, in the world of men, the two ' shadows ' Life and Death, he views them now as the servants of Love.

THE LESSON OF GRIEF, p. 148.

¹ 'Which ages thought of happy times'=which makes us feel old when we think of the happy times gone by. 'Ages' is a verb.

WIND ON THE LYRE, p. 148.

The 'Father-singer' of Ariel, the spirit in *The Tempest*, is Shakespeare, who was neither optimist nor pessimist, but poet. 'Green' and 'blue' are commonly used by Meredith to denominate 'earth' and 'heaven,' whose 'marriage' is a favourite theme in his poems. The farther the sound travels through the sky, the more it seems to dwell in our hearts.

TO COLONEL CHARLES, pp. 150-152.

A plea for steady, systematic armament, instead of laxity varied by fits of panic, a theme frequently recurring in these poems. Colonel Charles, to whom the poem is addressed, had witnessed the destruction of unprepared Austria's army at Königgrätz, the great Prussian victory of 1866. Chlum (xii) was the village in the centre of the Austrian position, wrapped that day in jets of smoke. The 'poet' referred to (ix) is Homer; the famous phrase quoted occurs in Od. xix. 13 and elsewhere.

THE CALL, pp. 156-157.

¹ *Exercitus* is Germany, the European power with the strongest army (1908). *The Salsipotent* is Britain, the sea-power. This poem is written in favour of universal military service.

FRANCE—DECEMBER 1870, pp. 158-165.

'France—December 1870' was written actually in that month, when the Germans were round Paris, and were covering eastern France with their 'league-long chains' of armies.

¹ Referring to the French Revolution, 1789.

² This section (v) refers to the first Napoleon's armies of seventy years before, whose violences and conquests are now being punished, remembered by the remorseless memories of the gods.

³ The rest of this section refers to the revival of superstition, and the rush to the churches to supplicate 'miraculous' deliverance from the Prussians. But the 'Mother of Reason' and of 'the many Laughters,' the land of Voltaire, can surely not expect much from that, says the poet.

⁴ Her 'Dishonour' ('Dishonourer' in first edition) means Napoleon iii.

THE VITAL CHOICE, p. 166.

Artemis and Aphrodite each claim all from Youth, who must give to each her dues, but not more. If we 'shun' either goddess, or 'too devoutly follow' either, they point us to Death. 'The Huntress' is

Artemis (Diana), Greek goddess of chastity and hunting—symbol here of our development of body, brain, and spirit in purity, in strife with the elements.

WITH THE HUNTRESS, pp. 166-168.

The picture is that of Artemis (who was goddess of the moon as well as of hunting and chastity) hunting by night through the forest-clad mountains.

INDEX OF FIRST LINES